Between Heaven And Hell – A Privileged Life

Angie Freeland

© Angie Freeland 2014

All rights reserved

No part of this publication may be reproduced, stored in a retrieval system, or transmitted in any form or by any means, without the prior permission in writing of the publisher, nor be otherwise circulated in any form of binding or cover other than that in which it is published and without a similar condition including this condition being imposed on the subsequent purchaser.

All paper used in the printing of this book has been made from wood grown in managed, sustainable forests.

ISBN: 978-1-78003-794-3

Printed and published in the UK

Pen Press is an imprint of
Author Essentials Ltd
4 The Courtyard
South Street
Falmer
BN1 9PQ

A catalogue record of this book is available from the British Library

Cover design by Jacqueline Abromeit

The events described in this book are true subject to the limitations of my memory which is not perfect by any means. All the events I have experienced personally are factual. Often I have written about what I have been told by others who have been material to the events in my life. These are opinions and remain so with no knowledge to be able or intention to present them as facts. I have also represented my opinions about what may have happened in order to make sense of facts I know to be true during various events in my life. These remain personal opinions with no intention to present them as fact. The people I have written about are real although their names in the book have been changed unless I have been given specific approval by those concerned to use their real names. I do not accept responsibility or liability for any indirect consequences to those individuals whose real names do not appear in the book.

Dedications

I dedicate this book to my husband Keith for always being there for me, never letting me down and for all the support you've given me throughout our 32 years together. You are my rock. Also to our son and daughter for the love and support you gave me throughout all the challenging times we've had. You both make my life complete. Thank you.

A special dedication to my mum and sister in spirit for all your love, guidance and support.

Acknowledgements

Thank you to all my family and friends that support me in all I want to do, you've motivated me and kept me going when I was feeling down and lost. Special thanks to my brother for keeping me safe when I was young and to my two nieces for standing by my side when the going got tough. Also to Lyn who saved my life, to Fran for listening and Sharron and Paul for inspiring and motivating me. Thank you all for believing in me more than I ever believed in myself.

A special thanks to Paul Page Photography in Sussex whose inspiring work features on the front and back covers and in the photograph section. Also to Peter Evers for the Irish Ghosthunters picture.

Foreword

Many people have said how they wish I would write a book sharing my experiences of life and my journey that led me to become a medium, and for a long time I thought about it, but always believed that no-one would be interested in little old me and what I had to say. However, the requests became more and more frequent, so I decided that maybe it was time to grab the bull by the horns and go for it. So here goes!

Introduction

So many people have asked me when I first realised that I could connect with spirit. Well, the answer to that is, when I was in my forties. I was a late starter when I finally allowed myself the beauty of connecting with spirit and realising I was able to communicate with them. You see from a very young age I was able to sense spirit around me, and throughout my life at different times I was able to receive messages from them, but for many reasons that I now realise were stupid reasons, I never allowed myself to develop my abilities any further. I feel so sad when I reflect on this now because I think of the many years that spirit had tried to work with me, and all I did was shun them like they weren't there.

I was born in the East End of London in 1961 to Irish Catholic immigrant parents who came over to England in the late 40s/early 50s to build a better life for themselves. Although my parents were both Irish they in fact met in Kilburn, London. Life wasn't easy for them when they first set out, or for us kids for that matter. But then I think that was pretty much the same for most people living in that era, especially those who lived in the East End of London.

I was brought up in a place called Hackney, London for the first decade of my life, then we moved to another area of London called Stamford Hill. I was the youngest of three siblings, my brother being the eldest, my sister being the middle child (something she hated), and me being the youngest. My father was an alcoholic and very abusive to Mum. By the time I was about six years old Mum had finally had enough of being in a bad marriage so she decided to divorce him. And what a great job she did of standing on her own two feet with three kids to bring up. Not an easy task, as I'm sure many of you will appreciate, especially back in those days.

Mum was 16 years old when she came over to England full of hope for her future, but what she didn't realise however, was that the Irish were very often treated like second class citizens, and life was going to be tougher than she could have imagined. Well for the first few years anyway. At that time things were still very fragile between the English and the Irish, as it had been for many, many years. The roots of this resentment and bitterness between the two countries stemmed right back to medieval times along with the low opinion the English and Irish had of each other. The story goes that the English distrusted all Irish, but in particular they had a real thing against the Irish Catholics, more because they wouldn't give up their religion and conform to becoming Protestants; they suffered greatly for this. Unfortunately these feelings of distrust would run through the veins of every generation on both sides for a long time to come. Thankfully things have now changed and people have become aware how Irish immigrants experienced more discrimination, racism, and prejudice through the ages than any other ethnic minority in areas such as employment, health, education, and housing. And I am just so pleased to see that, on the whole this kind of discrimination is no longer experienced to the level it was.

My parents were just two of the many thousands that have migrated over the decades to a different country looking for a better life. I just wonder how frightening that must have been for the likes of them. Especially when you think that most of the Irish came over on their own, which meant little or no support when they arrived. How quickly their hopes and dreams would have been shattered when they saw signs like 'No Blacks, No Irish and No Dogs' in the windows of boarding houses when they were trying to look for accommodation. I hate to think of my mum going through all of that. It must have been awful to have felt so unwelcome in a country that she hoped to start a new life in, and being so young too. It really doesn't bear thinking about.

My parents were classed as 'post war migrants' who had come over to England hoping to find work and were willing to do any kind of job they had to for survival. Mum ended up being a maid when she first arrived. It was certainly a hard life, but it was still better prospects than Ireland had to offer at that time. Mum once told me she really believed that the streets of London were paved with gold until she came over to live here that is. She shared with me a few times how lonely and isolated she felt in the early years, which is probably why she ended up living in Kilburn to start with as there has always been a very strong Irish community there, which would have been a great support to her, especially at the toughest times in her life. Bless her, even though she worked hard, made a good life for herself and was finally accepted into her community it did have a huge affect on her, and I can't help but wonder if that was why she always seemed so concerned about what other people thought of us as a family, what we looked like and why she had such a need to fit in. I'll never really know the answers to these questions, but I know my thoughts on it… Against all the odds Mum was determined to make it work and find happiness in her adopted country.

And find happiness she did. After divorcing my real father because she couldn't take any more abuse, Mum did find happiness, the happiness she had longed for and a week before my ninth birthday mum married my stepfather Peter. Although Pete, (who I shall refer to as dad from here on) was a good man, he had very strong beliefs on many subjects including religion and God. He was a total non-believer, and he certainly didn't believe in life after death. 'When you're gone, you're gone,' he used to always say. Although in the last few years of his life he started to be a bit more open minded and I realised for the very first time that perhaps his strong opinionated views about 'life after death' were all a bit of a ploy to hide his true beliefs. Remember, this was back in the 60s when it still wasn't OK to openly admit that you believed in something that had very little proof of existence. Maybe if the truth be known, dad didn't want to be seen as crazy either!

So here I was being brought up first in a Catholic household where your beliefs were shamed if you believed in anything other than your faith, and then, Mum goes and marries a man who not only didn't believe in spirit, but also didn't believe in God or religion! Needless to say all of these strong views, beliefs and high principles around me would totally scare the hell out of me because of what I was experiencing. I mean after all, here was little old me sensing spirit, having little chats with them and hearing things that went bump in the night. Oh boy was it hard to live in a household full of such strong beliefs and views, and each being at the opposite end of the scale, with very little balance in the middle. It's no wonder I thought I was going mad, felt different and didn't want to share what I was learning about spirit in fear of being mocked. As I look back now I remember the different kinds of arguments, including arguments about religion that took place in our household and how funny it seems to me now. Although at the time it was far from funny as the arguments could get very heated and loud which used to upset me so much.

Our family was certainly a confusing one, that's for sure. The dynamics that took place between everyone was a great recipe for confusion and denial. Mind you it wasn't all doom and gloom, and I don't want to paint that picture because there were some great times too, and I have such fond memories of those bygone years.

But you know, for all of the challenges, doubts, fears, and confusions that I went through, I wouldn't have had it any other way. I know that may sound really strange but it's true. They made me realise that I had to stand up for what's right for me and being true to myself. All that I went through taught me no matter what happens in life, our spirit can only be broken if we allow it to be. And, yes my friends, we do find the strength and courage we need to get through and overcome our darkest moments.

I hope you enjoy reading my story and the challenges I went through, which has brought me onto my life path now. I feel so honoured and proud to be a vessel for spirit, and I'll always be so grateful to them for never leaving my side and giving me the privilege of hearing their stories.

Chapter 1

THE EARLY YEARS

The first memory that I have of knowing that spirit was with me was around the age of six when I used to feel that someone other than my family members were with me. This was only a feeling at the time, I couldn't see anyone but I could definitely feel their presence, and at times was able to hear them. This feeling was always very strong which at first used to be quite scary, particularly as not only was I able to sense their presence but I was also able to hear them, and sometimes the bangs they made, or the call of my name could to me, be so loud that all I wanted to do was put my head under the pillows and hope they would go away. The fact that I was brought up in the Catholic faith which has the belief that there's no such thing, as spirit didn't help because it left me feeling very alone. I do have to say though in fairness to Mum, she wasn't a devout catholic, but obviously her beliefs were that of the faith she had been brought up to believe and had, to my knowledge, never questioned those beliefs. So from a very young age spirit became a part of my life, but knowing that spirit existed also began a path of inner conflict that travelled with me until I was in my forties.

The feelings, sounds and the voices I was hearing didn't go away. In fact they grew stronger, and because I was ashamed to share this with anyone I learnt to keep it all to myself. Quite a task for a six year old really, and believe me it was a very hard thing to do. So very often I used to hear my name being called and the voices were rarely the same, and I just didn't know if I should answer them, or even how to. Remember I was only six and I didn't have anyone to turn to.

As time went on I was able to feel the presence of spirit and hear them, but now I was also able to see what appeared to be shadows around me, or I would see someone out of the corner of my eye moving around. At that time I didn't know if they were male or female, good or bad, related to me or not, but I did know for sure they were spirit, and funnily enough as scary as this all was, I never questioned the fact that they had a right to be there. Again, I just learnt to deal with this, but I was still very young and had created many fears about all of this being my imagination and our religious faith didn't help that, but somehow deep down I always had a sense of knowing that these experiences were very real, which confused me even more. So there was a part of me that wanted all this to stop and a very big part of me that didn't, and one thing was for sure, I always knew that I was never on my own, which gave me great comfort through my loneliest of times. Even if I couldn't always see anyone, just feeling them around me was comforting in itself.

But there were also some very confusing times when I thought spirit was around me, when in fact it was a residual haunting. In other words the spirit wasn't around me to communicate with me, they were merely carrying on with what would have been their normal habits when they were alive, and it would be the same time every night. It's a bit like a film that's being run, and re-run. As an adult I came to understand that a residual haunting that happens like clockwork is merely a psychic imprint of the building replaying an event, or perhaps because of some trauma that was connected to the house or land that creates it, or the person living in it that creates it.

One of the most vivid memories I have of what I thought was spirit making their presence known to me was every night on the dot of 10.10 pm, and the sound of the front door being opened and then shut again, almost like someone coming home from work at the same time every evening. I could set my clock by it. What I didn't realise, and what I didn't find out until years later from my sister was that my mum very often used to see a shadow in the doorway at around the same time I used to hear the front door open and close. I do have to say though that I never spoke to my mum about this, so I can't confirm this 100 percent but my sister wouldn't have a reason to lie to me. What was really frustrating for me was that if I heard the door open and close and noises of someone walking around, why weren't they showing themselves to me? Or calling my name like the other spirits did?

Obviously as my abilities developed in my latter years I realised the difference was because ghosts who run and re-run their habits from their time here on earth are not aware of our presence, nor are they wanting to communicate with us, they're just doing their thing. Spirit however, are there because they want to communicate with us, they want to guide us, give us a message, or tell us their story. Yep they are always there for a reason. They are classed as intelligent spirit.

Anyway, back to what I was saying. I can remember feeling so relieved that someone else in the family was aware of the things that were happening in our home. For the first time ever I didn't feel so alone. The house that we lived in until I was 13 years old was a Victorian end of terrace corner house, so obviously it had had many occupants and of course it was old and creaky, especially back then when most houses, including ours, didn't have the luxury of central heating or double glazing. Well at least not in the early part of my life anyway, and yet I knew what I was experiencing wasn't all what I now understand to be residual haunting. No, far from it! I have to say I truly loved this house and saw it very much as my home, ghosts and spirits included and they became very much a part of my family.

None of the spirits that used to visit me were ever there to harm me or any of my family, but because of my lack of understanding at this time there was a fear inside of me that believed they might. I really laugh when I think of this now, because as I have learnt through the experiences with spirit they have more than proved to me that it is not their reason for communicating with us.

My experiences of sensing spirit around didn't just happen at home. It would also happen when I was in others homes or even in public places. Now that was scary! I can remember even in my primary school, that I often used to stand outside the school looking up at it, knowing that there were still many spirits visiting, and all for their own reasons. So you see it seemed to be stepping up and happening wherever I used to be.

When spirit first started to let me know they were with me, it was through my feelings. I always felt they were there first, but I so desperately wanted to see them just once to confirm that my feelings and this knowing I had were real. I wanted it confirmed that I wasn't crazy, because there were so many times I really did wonder if it was me. But that wasn't to happen for some time to come. However the sense of feeling and knowing of their presence was getting stronger and as I was growing older I felt very alone and had no support to help me realise what was happening to me and that it wasn't my imagination. It had started to worry me why no-one ever talked about having the same kind of experiences. I honestly got to the point that I thought something was wrong with me, and because of the religious faith within my family and the beliefs about heaven and hell I also felt very shameful that I could even believe that life after death did exist. Was I being bad for believing in something that I knew was around me, that I was being told doesn't exist? Did this mean that I would go to hell instead of heaven? So the whole thing of being damned came into play for me. Not nice for any child to experience. I have to say, now, as an adult my spiritual path has, thankfully, brought me to the belief that we are all under one roof, and when we pass over into the light we are not judged or segregated because of our actions or beliefs whilst we're here on the physical plane. For me, there is no heaven or hell, just our spiritual home on another plane waiting to welcome us back, and when we return we are helped and counselled by our Elders, Guides and the Love of the Divine on what we have learned through the life we have just led, and how, should we choose to return we can balance out karma and evolution for the greatest and highest good; but more about that later. Of course the other big bonus is that when we have returned back to our spiritual home, we are once again reunited with our loved ones.

As you can imagine this was a difficult time for me what with of all of these concerns and worries about heaven, hell, right or wrong, and to make matters worse, I had gone from sensing spirit around me to being able to see shadows forming, moving and disappearing very quickly. Things were definitely changing. It really started to feel that if I got used to one change, another one was waiting in the wings to make another step in and strengthen my abilities even further. Not that I saw it like that at the time. No, definitely not. For me, all these changes were freaky, scary, and confusing. As I could have predicted, the next change wasn't too far around the corner.

I had started to hear my name being called very frequently and normally at night when I was alone in my bedroom. At first this scared me as much as the shadows did, but after a while, I found the voices calling me quite comforting. But you know what scared me even more was the fact that no one else in the family appeared to be experiencing the same things. Or at least they weren't saying anything to me. It all sounds a bit sinister as I write this, what with the shadows, hearing voices, and things that go bump in the night, but it wasn't. I know now that the shadows were the residual haunting, and probably the things that went bump in the night were attached to that also, and the sensing and hearing voices were those on the other side of the veil trying to communicate with me.

As I grew older I realised that one my greatest concerns was not about spirit wanting to communicate with me, but more about what others would think of me if they knew what was happening. I was learning to fit into the social box of what was expected of me, how we should think and what we should believe. I really wasn't that worried about spirit being in my life, but I was worried about how I was going to fit into the mould that society was forming for me, and society's expectations didn't have room in it for spirit. This world didn't leave much room for the 'other side'. Well it wouldn't really because it would mean that this would take us out of the normal way of thinking, and for the high majority of those who were afraid of the unknown, this wasn't a comfortable place to be, because it can't be labelled or scientifically explained. Thankfully in today's world we can combine the two together with all the equipment that is now being used in paranormal investigations, which for me can help to blend the physical world and the spiritual realm together.

It's so sad really that at such a young age I had these kinds of worries and no support to get through it all because of society's expectations and the ridicule a person can go through just because a person has different beliefs. So because I was worried that I wouldn't fit into the world I was being brought up in, and although things were definitely getting stronger from my spiritual perspective, I still didn't have the confidence to say anything to others in fear of being judged.

By the time I was 13 there had been some big changes in our house. My brother Frank had left home joined the army and had got married. He was my hero when I was a child and could do no wrong in my eyes and I missed him so much, but to add to that my sister had also left home, got married and was starting a family of her own. For a while it felt a bit like I was an only child, which was nice in some ways but oh how I missed the arguments and the laughter that us siblings would have, and again that lonely feeling would raise its ugly head.

It was at this time my parents decided to move. Well, I say they had decided to move, it was more because there was a compulsory purchase order placed on every house in the street because the council wanted to build a new development there so we had to move. I was excited because I had always lived in the same house and I wanted the experience of living somewhere different and getting to know new people, and I also believed by moving I would be free of some of the terrible memories that were connected to certain people and that house. Memories that went onto haunt me for many years to come.

When my mum split up with my real father she didn't have any child support from him so she took in lodgers and ended up having a brief relationship with one lodger in particular called Dudley. I guess it must have been serious for Mum because she trusted him with us kids – Mum's mistake number two. The first one was getting involved with him in the beginning. Anyway as their relationship developed he became very much a part of our family. All was really good at first and he seemed to enjoy being around kids, and I've got to be honest, he was great fun to be around. Very often he used to join us in the street for a game of football and Mum certainly felt at ease leaving me with him. I was the youngest and still needed babysitting whereas my brother and sister were old enough to be out hanging around with their mates. I on the other hand was stuck with him and even though Mum didn't leave me often, on the occasions she did, yes, your mind is probably going in the right direction, he sexually abused me. All his being nice and wanting to be like a dad to me was him getting me to trust him.

From the very first moment he violated me, betrayed my trust, and took away the innocence of my childhood he left a scar that ran so deep and was going to take years to heal. It's so true when abuse victims say they 'feel dirty', because we do, and I know for me I felt so ashamed of what had happened, which created a guilt inside me that I carried around with me for years. You know I sometimes think the only way I could get to grips with what happened was to blame myself. After all, someone I trusted shouldn't do this to me. This thought rattled around in my head for years leaving me with a whole heap of emotions and feelings to deal with.

As always this was yet another secret to keep. I don't know why I didn't tell my mum or anyone else for that matter what had happened, but there was obviously a reason. I can't say I remember Dudley ever threatening to harm me if I told anyone, but somehow in some way there was a threat of some kind, otherwise it would have been easy to run to Mum and tell her. All I can remember is feeling scared, and all of a sudden life became more unsafe than it had ever been. Thankfully, the relationship between Mum and Dudley didn't last long, which meant he was out of my life for good. Or was he? What he had done had left me feeling very tarnished, not good enough for anyone. He had destroyed my trust in everyone and from the moment the abuse began I started to become very distant with those around me, even the people I loved and I wouldn't let anyone near me on an emotional level.

For many years all my relationships were affected, and I carried that guilt around for years until I met Keith, bless him. (Keith is my wonderful hubby of 29 years who has helped me through so much). As frustrating as he found this he wasn't going to give in, even if it did take many years before he felt like there was a breakthrough. Poor old Mum though, I never told her what had happened so all she knew was that she had a daughter who was becoming increasingly more difficult and rebellious with each day that dawned. I never could quite bring myself to hurt her by telling her. No it was best left unsaid. I often used to wonder what she would have done if she had known. Maybe I would have got the support I needed, who knows? But it's history now, Mum never did find out, so I'll never know. So moving away from a house that held so much both good and bad was so confusing. I had so much going around in my head. I was also worried that if we moved away those who were visiting me from spirit wouldn't be able to visit me anymore. In my young innocent eyes I honestly thought if we moved they wouldn't know where I was to visit me. Even though I was only young I knew that life wasn't ever going to be the same. But would it be better, worse or just different? Only time would tell.

From the very first night I spent in our new home I hated it. The new house was a rather large seven bedroom house with four floors, and my bedroom was right at the top of the house, which felt a bit cut off, and to add to that I didn't like the feeling of the house. It felt very unlucky to me. I also struggled to make friends in the area, and my school was a good four or five miles away from where we lived, so I wasn't really able to hang around with them after school. I think Mum was hoping that I would meet some new friends in the area and settle down but I didn't, mainly because there was a large orthodox Jewish community who didn't mix with anyone other than those who belonged to their faith. Of course, as a teenager I was struggling with the normal hormones and bad attitude, and the usual fighting internal demons of confusion and fears that many experience as we're developing into young adults, but it went beyond that.

For a long time there I felt very isolated in so many ways, and although at times I was still sensing spirits around me, it wasn't as frequent as it had previously been. I was still trying to be 'part of the crowd' and that meant not talking about spirits and my experiences, so, sadly I kept quiet. Oh I had many a chat with friends about 'ghosts' as we would call them then, but no-one ever mentioned having any experiences with them directly, it was just the usual typical stories or old wives tales that kids would hear from the people around them. I didn't realise it at the time, but I was closing down because of the stigma that was around people being able to 'talk to the dead', although, thankfully not completely as every now and then I would once again feel the presence of a lady or a gentleman around me. Oh, I had forgotten to say, by this time I was now able to gather a little more information from spirit with each connection, and I would still regularly hear my name being called. By this time I was able to decipher whether it was a male or female but I still didn't have a clue who it was. It could have been my grandparents or Gunga Din for all I knew. What I did know was that I had a real need to belong back then so even when I heard my name being called, I would either ignore them, or tell them to go away because in my eyes I needed to be the same as everyone else. How sad is that? I was prepared to let go of the wonderful connection I had with those who had passed. It was understandable because of my age etc., but very sad. Thankfully spirit wasn't going to take no for an answer. Bless them, spirit would leave me alone for a while, and then I would get a little reminder of some sort that they were still with me. I have to say how grateful I am to them for never leaving me, even though I gave them such a hard time.

At last as a teenager I had started to develop my own social life, and I was busy focusing on my future and by the age of 16 I had left school and was working for Burberrys as a trainee tailoress. Oh and I had discovered boys! One in particular, and before long we were 'going serious'.

These developing years were turbulent and chaotic for me, and gave me some very painful experiences as I was never able to express my feelings very well, so became quite an angry young woman. I was also confused about God and religion, and didn't really know what I believed in, except for one thing. I had absolutely no doubt that when we passed over we still existed, all be it on another dimension, and I never stopped believing that spirit were around me even though I didn't hear, feel or see them quite as much as I used to. I never doubted that they were there, guiding me through life, keeping me safe, even if at times it felt like I was being guided down a blind alley. Oh boy, did I give them a hard time for this, but they knew I didn't mean it, it was just me letting off steam and all my frustrations to those I trusted, and although I didn't realise it at the time, I did trust them.

I was being protected and cared for by my wonderful Spirit Guides, and all of those 'blind alleys' I felt like I was being taken down at the time was a necessary part of my journey. I came to realise that in fact it was mostly me taking me down those alleys as a result of the thoughts, actions and turmoil that I felt inside me, and it was my main spirit guide, Jed, who was bringing me back on the right path, though many a time I would come back kicking and screaming. You see we all have a guide that is assigned to us from birth, and they will be with us throughout every situation in our life. Now, these guides will have the job of keeping us on the true path of our destiny, but as we all know, the problem with us humans is that although we have choices in every situation, a lot of the time we tend to choose the most difficult path, and it becomes the job of our guide to ensure that not only do we learn from this experience but they will also guide us back onto our right path. For me, Jed keeps me well and truly on the straight and narrow, and I am so grateful for his love, care and the wisdom that he shares with me so often. I hate to think what life would be like if he wasn't with me. There are many great books out there about our spirit guides and how you can meet them and I would recommend anyone to have a read of them, as they can be so enlightening. You never know, maybe that's the next book for me!

Anyway, back to what I was saying. My experiences throughout my younger years were a very necessary part of my path, and through these sometimes painful experiences I learned what was important for me. These years gives us the opportunity to build our life according to our views and beliefs, and although we may not recognise it then, or in my case for many years to come, I believe somewhere deep down inside, we will hold what's right for us. Whether we're aware of it or not life and its coincidences will lead us into the direction of where we can uphold and live by these views even if sometimes it means travelling on a bumpy road.

In my eyes our guides and spirit are wonderful and I'm so glad that I eventually found the courage to speak out and say, 'Yes, there is life after death,' and 'Yes, I communicate with spirit and I'm proud of it.' Each and every one of my experiences in life made me realise just how important spirit are to me, and instead of shunning spirit I'm always so glad when they are near me. I will never stop wanting to hear their story because each and every spirit that communicates with me has a story to tell, and not only do I want to hear it, I want to share it as well.

Chapter 2

GOING AGAINST THE GRAIN

By the time I was 20 years old I was starting to realise that I was not going to be a follower of any one religious faith. My belief at that point was that there is something out there other than us humans that is connected to us all. Something so beautiful and divine that cannot be placed under any one religion, something that we are all a part of and share. Now, as a 52 year old this beautiful source for me is the divine source that's connected to the universe and us and is the greater love for all. For me the divine is not a male/female taking control but a loving energy that not only do we always have all around us, but also we have within us. That part of us that loves unconditionally, wants to be of service to others, and whose actions and thoughts are in complete harmony with the energy that surrounds us, and is within us. Everything and everyone that we see and hear in this world is part of all of this, for we are one. We are never separated from this source, and we need to remember this in our troubled times. This divine energy hears our prayers, answers them and guides us through our toughest times, never judging or shaming us for when we get it wrong, and we will get it wrong you know because we're human and that's what we do. Forgive me if I haven't explained this very well, because to me there are no words that could describe the wonder of my divine God. I also believe that when we open our hearts, not only to all that is within this physical world and allow ourselves to go beyond and sense, feel, see and hear what is on another dimension, we open up to all that is possible. By doing this we can connect with our guides as well as those we have loved that have passed on the other side of the veil. And it doesn't stop there!

Anyway getting back to when I was 20 years old. So I had decided to go against all that I had been brought up to believe in, to go against all that didn't feel right for me. That went against the grain in more ways than one in my family, as I had started to express my beliefs quite openly, although at times it would be in a somewhat aggressive way. Well, I was only young and was really finding my feet at living by and expressing my beliefs. Now don't get me wrong, I have the utmost respect for all religions and faiths, and also for every individual who has different beliefs to myself, and I believe very strongly that we can each learn from each other's faiths and beliefs. After all, I think that spirituality and religion has many common beliefs, the main one being love and kindness to others.

There had been many changes for me between the ages of 16 and 20, and I had gone through my rebellious years of doing my own thing which, most of the time backfired on me quite badly, as half the time any decisions I made were normally out of anger and defiance and I normally ended up cutting off my nose to spite my face. For example getting married when I was 18 years old! I met my first husband, Stuart, when I was around the age of 15 and a half. I had already had a couple of boyfriends before then but to be honest it was more a question of hanging around together rather than going out with each other. Anyway occasionally I used to go to a social club with a couple my mum and dad was friendly with, their daughter who was roughly the same age as me. It wasn't really my cup of tea but it got me out for a few hours.

A few weeks before I met Stuart I had been asked out by a young man called Michael but had turned him down because he wasn't really my type. I had noticed him around the club a few times but that was mainly because he was such a great dancer. But I didn't find him good looking. I had never seen him hanging around with anyone before so I didn't realise he had a brother. I can remember the first time I saw Stuart. 'Hmm, not bad,' I quietly said to myself, and the next thing I know he's coming over to join our crowd. It turned out he knew my mum's friends and by the end of the evening he had asked me out. I knew even then that there was no chemistry between us, and to this day I don't know why I said yes, but I did. I don't think his brother Michael was too pleased! And boy, did he let us know it. As we said goodnight I gave him my phone number so he could call me to set up a date. That non trusting part of me didn't think he would call, and to be honest at that stage I didn't really care, but to my surprise the phone did ring a few days later and I knew the voice at the other end was Stuart when he said, 'Is that Angie?'

Of course, I played dumb and pretended I didn't know who it was. 'Yeah it is; who's that?' I asked in an abrupt tone.

'It's Stuart; I promised I would ring you. Now before we talk about going out for a drink I want to know if you're on the up.'

I was gob smacked! What the hell did he mean? I had started to feel annoyed by this phone call and I think he could tell by the tone of my voice when I said, 'What do you mean am I on the up?' I could tell we were already starting to spark off of each other.

'I mean you haven't got another bloke in tow?'

'You bloody cheeky git! Of course I haven't; what kind of girl do you take me for?' The hackles on my back were up and at that point I didn't really want to see this bloke again, but by the end of the phone call we had arranged to go out for a drink the following night. And for any of you who has clicked that I was 15 years old and was drinking, yep, I was! Back then in the East End a lot of us teenagers started to grow up very young, and I was one of them. It was a very common thing in our area to be out drinking at such an early age, and back then we never got asked for identification, or how old we were; the laws were very lax. When I think back now, how different life was then. I wasn't even 16 years old and I had started work at Burberrys as a trainee tailoress and was also working at a bar at night. God, we used to get away with so much – you wouldn't be able to do that now!

I realised very early on that the relationship with Stuart wasn't going to last. We didn't have much in common and it was very volatile. If we went three days without having a row we were lucky. So why did I keep seeing him? I knew I didn't love him, and I knew he loved me very much. Habit. It's a bit like smoking really, I knew it wasn't good for me, but I kept on doing it because it became a habit I would be lost without. And in those times it was quite normal to meet your partner, get engaged and married all by the age of 20, well at least where I came from anyway. I also think there was a part of me spiting my mum by staying with him because she couldn't stand him and very frequently made her feelings known. But for all that, she was great when we got engaged. However the closer we got to setting a date, the more Mum started to give me a hard time until in the end we decided to get a special license and three days later we were married without anyone knowing. Now all I had to do was tell my mum!

As I predicted she hit the roof! 'I thought I would have had at least one of yous here to help me,' were her words once she got over the shock. I must admit those words went around in my brain for a long time, and I couldn't help but wonder if that's all I was good for. It certainly felt like it at the time. Once I broke the news to her I hastily packed my bags, got out of the line of her fire and moved in with my new husband's family. Big mistake! I hated it there and I realised very quickly I had made what felt like the biggest mistake of my life. I started to regret getting married almost immediately, and I could see that all I really wanted was freedom and to be respected for being an adult, and yet all my behaviours were shouting out that in fact I was far from being an adult and was very much still a child who was lost and trying to find her way.

Our marriage started to break down very quickly, and in no time at all I wanted out. Mum wasn't helping things either because all she kept saying to me every time she saw me was, 'It will never last,' and putting pressure on me to see sense.

Of course she was right. By our first wedding anniversary we had split up very much to Mum's relief. Even that was funny though because Mum was in Ireland visiting family when I finally walked out on Stuart, and naturally I confided in my sister that I had left him. We were due to speak to Mum that night and Lu-Lu begged me to let her be the one to tell Mum instead of me. I found this strange because I thought Mum would want to hear it from me, but I gave in as usual and let her do it. Anything for a quiet life!

So after my brief spell of married life I returned home with my tail between my legs, and naturally I had to eat a lot of humble pie but in time Mum and I were starting to get on a lot better, and I was building up a great life as a single person again. But for as much as I had started to enjoy life again I always felt as though there was something missing. Something I had lost over these last few years. My connection with spirit! Although I think at the time I was quite relieved as I didn't feel I could cope with anything else on my plate, but as usual, at the same time I was missing their little visits and nudges to remind me they were there. However that was all about to change.

When I was 19 years old I had brief contact with my real father, John. I have to say it was brief because I couldn't really forgive him for the way he had treated Mum, and for deserting us children to meet his own needs in life all those years earlier, so as you can imagine I didn't get on with him very well. The poor man couldn't make amends even if he wanted to, because I wasn't in the place to allow him to. Again, I didn't share with Mum at first that I had met him because I knew she would go ballistic. He was someone that she just wanted to forget. Not an easy thing to do being as she had his three kids.

Anyway, one night while I was sleeping, I heard my real father calling me, and the next thing I knew I was in a hospital with him. There he was standing there in a pair of pyjamas, waiting to greet me. I didn't want to talk to him, but I knew I had to listen, and he gave me a message to pass onto my mum which was, 'Look after your mother for me, she was the only woman I every truly loved.' Once he gave me this, he started to float away, and as he did he told me how sorry he was for everything. I could hear his voice echoing in my ears, and I can remember watching him float away out of sight. I knew I wasn't asleep, I knew it wasn't a dream, but I really couldn't work out what had just happened. This put me in a state of shock and although I was questioning what had just happened, I really knew deep down that it wasn't a dream, and that my father really had come to me with a message and to say goodbye. I knew he had passed and I believe it was at the very moment he came to me to make sure Mum knew he loved her.

It was quite nice really to know that Mum was the last person he thought of before he passed. Mum deserved that, but how on earth was I going to pass this message onto Mum from him knowing how she felt about 'His Lordship'? (As we nicknamed him because Mum never used to like us calling him Dad or James) And especially as I had no proof to give her to support what I was telling her, just what I had experienced. I was dreading it but I knew I had to do it. So I braced myself and choose an opportune moment when we were alone and she was in a good mood. To my surprise Mum was very willing to listen to me, and afterwards she told me that he had constantly been on her mind for the last few days, and couldn't shake him off.

Although we didn't say it to each other at the time, we both found it significant that she had been thinking of him over the last few days, and I had this message to pass on. We both knew he had passed but finding out for sure was going to be the hardest part, as we had no idea of where he had been living since the last time I saw him. I had lost contact with anyone that knew him during my brief reunion with him a few years earlier. But I also think we were both afraid of opening up a can of worms if we did try to find out. So we decided to let it go and get on with life. But for me, what had happened was so powerful and amazing that I couldn't get it out of my mind. I had received my first true message, and I wanted more experiences like that. I spent many nights asking for him to come back and communicate with me again.

A few months had passed and no more was said between Mum and I, and then one day I ran into an old friend of my real father's called Henry. Henry would from time to time meet up with James and come to London to visit his old haunts. Naturally I asked him if he had heard from my dad. His answer didn't surprise me at all when he told me that he had heard that my father had passed away a few months before, and he assumed I would have heard the news. Not that I needed any real convincing that my father had visited me that night, but if I did, then this was it!

This message wasn't only important on a personal level, but also from a mediumistic perspective because it had gone onto another stage. This time I didn't just sense spirit with me, or hear my name being called, but I had actually received a message, and I saw him and knew whom it was from. That incredible feeling of knowing that spirit can still reach out, can still send their love, heal, and help bring closure even though they're no longer on this earth. This experience made my beliefs even stronger than before, but now I wanted not only to see, hear, feel them, but I wanted to be able to ask them questions and communicate with them properly. I was so frustrated. Where do I turn to? Who can I speak to? There was no-one. No-one that I could learn from, no-one that could hold my hand and lead me on the path to developing what I had been experiencing. But for all of these challenges, deep down inside me there must have been a part of me that believed I wouldn't have been given the opportunity to experience spirit if there wasn't a reason, but why did it have to be so hard? Why did I have to wait for so long? Grrrrrr!

Although not a tremendous amount changed as a result of the connection I had with my father, the good thing for me was that they were back, even if, at that time I didn't quite know how to work with them. I felt so comforted that they were still around me.

So the little ways that spirit chose to let me know they were around me still continued, but sadly there was still no huge revelations and still no support, but I had got to the point where I had stopped letting that worry me, and I had almost resigned myself to the fact that this was how it was always going to be. Plus, when I was 21 years old, the most wonderful man I had ever met had come into my life. (That sounds so slushy, but so true). Of course I'm talking about my lovely husband Keith. Talk about having a sense of knowing. I knew the night I met Keith that I was going to marry him, all I had to do was get divorced first! That sounds so funny as I write it, but it's true.

Our relationship was very passionate and strong from the beginning, and in no time we were living together, getting engaged and when I was 23 years old we got married. Oh we've had our ups and downs over the years as we all do in relationships, but it was definitely the best decision I had ever made, and here we are 30 years later still together, and still as strong as ever. And the family not only approved of my choice but loved Keith and welcomed him into our family with open arms. Yay! At last Mum approved and Keith could do no wrong in her eyes.

Keith had a very scientific mind, in fact he studied physics and in the beginning of his career he worked for BP as a lab technician. So in Keith's mind there was always a rational answer for everything. How was I going to share my experiences with him? He would think I was crazy. Oh he knew I believed very strongly in spirit and that I used to visit mediums from time to time, but he didn't realise just how deep it went for me, although every so often I would give him little snippets of something that I had experienced. I can remember doing this on one occasion when we visited some friends who had an apartment in an old renovated mansion. I could sense a dominant male around me every time I went there, and I knew he was watching us all. He definitely wanted our attention. Well he got mine!

Now you're probably thinking with all of the encounters I was having with spirit, why didn't I try communicating with them by asking them what they wanted. Or how could I help them? Well, the answer to that is easy. Firstly, although I knew I had the ability to feel, see, hear them, and know they were there, I didn't think for one minute that I had the ability to communicate in a way that I would get answers. I always just took it that the spirit was there first, had a connection to either the land or building I was in at the time and they were very wary of anyone that came into it. After all I was in their space. Oh if only I had the experience and knowledge that I have now. I could have found out so much from them, and helped them if I could have. Anyway back to this dominant gentleman in my friend's home.

Whenever we went there I would react every time because I knew he would be waiting for me. (That's how I felt about it at the time.) I did share with Keith that I felt someone was with us, and I knew it was a male, and I also shared with my friend who lived there what happened every time I visited her, and to my surprise she told me that she often felt his presence, and on a number of occasions had told him to go away. Keith could see how I was behaving when we were there, but he didn't really take it seriously, but that's not his fault, that's my fault because I wasn't being open enough to say how serious this all was for me, and I hadn't shared any of the past experiences that had gone on throughout my life. So why would he take it seriously when I wasn't. So sure enough it all turned into a bit of a joke when we visited them, and as always he would be there waiting and watching us. Thankfully he never took it any further than that, otherwise I think I may well have freaked at that time. I never did get to the bottom of what the spirit wanted because we moved away.

So the little connections with spirit were continuing, and in fact had started to increase slightly, and frequently; for instance, when we visited Keith's mum and dad. When I walked into their home for the first time I felt an elderly gentleman around me, and very often when I used to be alone upstairs to go to the loo or if we were staying there I would feel this presence getting stronger. As I look back, what is interesting is that without realising it at the time I was tuning in more and more, and receiving more and more information from spirit. For example I knew this gentleman was elderly; I knew that he had lived in this house, and I felt as though he had died there, things that were confirmed to me later. One of the things that was significant was that apart from the connection I had with my real father, none of the spirit I sensed around me were personally connected to me, or at least I didn't think so at the time, but who knows?

So I had conformed, and on the surface I was able to do this without too many problems. Heck, I had even started going to church in our village in Aberdeen, and Keith and I even became Sunday school teachers for a while (something that surprised everyone, including me). But at last I was fitting in, and for the first time in a long time I felt truly part of a community, something I hadn't experienced feeling since we moved from our little Victorian house in Hackney when I was 13 years old. But was I happy? In most ways yes, but not completely. By this I mean as much as I loved living there I still hadn't found fulfilment. I was being haunted by so much of my past and I couldn't seem to come to terms with all that had happened and move on. As I said earlier, on the surface it seemed to all those around me that I had settled down and had started to live life on the right track. After all, here I was married to the most wonderful man who treated me right and made me feel so special, and yet inside I was a wreck. The truth was the abuse, my first marriage, the way I had treated Stuart and all the other things that had affected my self worth were haunting me. I had never had much self worth but it seemed now that I was in a 'safe' relationship with a man I adored, and I had stopped fighting the world, I was falling apart. I felt tarnished, dirty, insecure and not worthy of all that I had. My nerves were in a terrible state, my anxiety levels had shot through the roof and I had lost interest in everything, not because I wanted to but because I just didn't have the energy for anything, including eating. My weight was going down to nothing and all in all I was a real mess. The nightmares had started again, and they were always the same kind. Someone chasing me and I couldn't escape. They had started after the abuse had taken place and were to continue periodically right up until I was in my forties. This time I couldn't sweep all this under the carpet and forget; no, this time I had to do something about it before I destroyed myself and my marriage to Keith.

Poor old Keith was struggling to cope with me, and I didn't know how to deal with what was happening to me myself, so the first port of call was the doctors. Back then the answer to anxiety or depression was tablets. No offers of counselling and we certainly couldn't afford to pay privately for me to see a counsellor so I started taking the medication. The problem was the tablets weren't having much of an effect on me and I was getting worse. I felt spaced out all the time, and I felt alone, mainly due to me isolating myself, and over a period of a few weeks the cracks were really starting to show. It even got to the point where I was struggling to hold down the little part time job I had in a newsagent's. I couldn't explain how I felt to anybody because I didn't really know myself apart from the fact that I felt like I wanted to fall asleep and never wake up. Keith and I battled along like this for months without telling anyone, and I was just sinking lower and lower into depression, but in the end I just couldn't take it any longer and in a desperate attempt to stop feeling the way I did I ended up taking an overdose. Did I want to die? Looking back now I can see I didn't really want to, I just didn't want to wake up to the way I was feeling every day. It was such a relief to be in hospital, and to finally be receiving the help that I so desperately needed and Keith was a tower of strength as always. It must have been so difficult for him to see his wife hitting rock bottom the way I did. The doctor in charge of my case was brilliant, and instead of being hard on me for doing such a stupid thing he was totally the opposite. 'Mrs Freeland I think it's best if you are admitted to a psychiatric hospital for us to get to the bottom of this and give you the help that you need.' I was more than happy to do anything he wanted me to do as long as I got better.

Once I had been transferred to the psychiatric hospital it wasn't long before they diagnosed intrinsic depression, which I understand to be a depression that hasn't been brought on by any one external cause but a build up of stress and how a person deals with this stress inwardly, which can create a chemical imbalance. So here was I thinking I had dealt with all my past life's issues and moved on when in fact all I had done was to store them up, lock the feelings away and act like nothing was wrong, which had affected me in more ways than one, including the chemical balance in my body. I didn't really understand all of this when they were telling me and I'm not sure I fully understand it all now, but I do remember feeling as though something was finally being done to help lift me out of this dark hole that I had become so familiar with.

Of course, what I didn't realise was that getting better meant facing my inner demons. Facing and feeling all that I had locked away for many years, all the things that had hurt me but I had never actually spoken about or dealt with. There were some days when it actually felt good to talk and let things go, then there were times when I felt like crap after my counselling session and would cry for days, and there were other times when I couldn't even discuss some of the things that I had locked away. I realised very quickly this was going to take a long time, but I didn't realise how long!

You know the strangest thing was here I was in a psychiatric hospital being treated for depression because I had basically had a breakdown, and I hadn't told my mum or the rest of my family. Keith had told his mum, dad and brother, but between them they had decided not to tell anyone else so that it wouldn't be too hard for me when I came home. But I hadn't told my mother because I didn't want her to feel ashamed of me and I didn't want to hurt her because some of the things I had bottled up were things that happened when I was a child. So each week when we were due to have our weekly phone call (remember Mum lived in Ireland and we lived in Scotland) I used to pretend that everything was OK, and talk about surface stuff. To my knowledge she never really picked up that anything was wrong, and I never did tell her, mainly because I didn't see the point.

I was in hospital for about two weeks, and by the time I was released I felt like I was back in the land of the living once more, although I wasn't under any illusions – the hard work had only just started. Getting back into the swing of things wasn't easy as I was still very tired and drained from all that I had been through physically, mentally and emotionally, but having said all that, I had started to feel an inner strength that wasn't there before, a strength that told me I was going to get through this, no matter what it took, and of course having Keith by my side to support me made all the difference. When I look back now and realise all that I went through it really feels like it happened to another person. Was I really this person that could crumble like that? It seems impossible now to even contemplate how low I had got, and how I had allowed the experiences in my life to break me like that. For a short while there my breakdown did crack my spirit within, but it couldn't break it, because my strength and determination within to survive all that had happened came from my spirit, my soul.

Always remember, my friends, just because life knocks you down at times, doesn't mean you can't get back up again, and I'm living proof of that!

Facing the inner demons that I had hidden for years was far more difficult than I ever could have possibly imagined, and there were times when I would have preferred things to be left alone, but I knew deep down that was me trying to avoid my feelings. It took years of therapy and hard work in coming to terms with some of the most painful experiences in my life and how it had all affected me, but I can say now with hand on heart that it was well worth it. I am no longer Dudley's victim. Or for that matter the victims of any other past hurts and challenges, and it's a wonderful feeling. Oh I know I will always have the scars, but as we all know, scars can heal.

It's funny really, but I never talk about this episode in my life. At first I think it was through the shame of it all, because if I'm truly honest I was very ashamed of 'cracking up' because of the stigma that's attached to it. Once people realise you have had a break down, depression or anxiety, you're forever labelled, either as mad, weak, strange, nutty or mentally retarded. These are some of the words I've heard other people say when describing someone who has had mental health issues. I was going to make sure I wasn't labelled like that. After all, I was still very vulnerable at that point, and because of the shame I was feeling at that time, I may well have taken it on board and believed it. Maybe there was a part of me at that time that believed I was mad. Hmm, as I sit with that one I realise that's how I did see myself! But now the reason I don't ever talk about it is because it's over, it's history, and it feel like it belongs to another lifetime. Do I still worry about what people think? Well, my friends, if I did, I wouldn't be writing about it in this book. All this took place about 26 years ago, so it doesn't actually matter anymore. In fact if anything I see this as one of the most positive things that's happened to me in my life, because it's only through hitting rock bottom and having to fight my way back up that I realised how precious life really is, and nothing, but nothing is worth taking our life over. And as for people labelling me, well, those who are important in my life have accepted me warts and all, and I accept myself for who I am, but if others want to judge me based on this episode in my life then maybe it's them who now needs to do some work on themselves.

But you know what I find really fascinating is that, not only were Irish immigrants and second generation Irish born in the UK the most bullied ethnic minority, albeit that the bullying was very subtle, there is also a clear indication that those children born to Irish immigrants have a higher rate of mental health issues and a higher rate of mortality, especially amongst females and when I researched this further I was really alarmed to see that second generation Irish show a higher rate of being smokers and suffering with heart disease. But it doesn't stop there. According to statistics once more, there's also proof that there appears to be a higher rate of physical illnesses. There are some that believe the reason for all of these health issues amongst the first generation Irish may be because they were not accepted when they arrived in England, the culture was very different, and let's not forget the racism that went on back in the 40s, 50s and 60s and as close as 1990s. As for the second generation all reports and statistics certainly indicates that a lot of the mental and physical health problems stems from not being accepted either in Ireland or in England. Going by my own experiences I can relate to that. The Irish didn't accept me, and the English certainly didn't as the bullying I experienced when I was at school taught me. Sadly, I learnt from a very young age that I was classed as a 'plastic paddy'. In other words I'm not real. Well, that was my perception of it anyway. So really and truly with all that rippling through society when I was growing up, is it any wonder I had the problems I had? And believe me it wasn't any comfort to find out that I wasn't mad, because it made me realise that there are so many others out there that have also been affected by the small mindedness of others and their judgemental attitudes. Hmm, a lot of food for thought here for any of you that have gone through the same kind of experiences.

But getting back to what I was saying. Before my health had declined so badly Keith and I had been talking about starting a family, and although for a while there it wouldn't have been the right thing to do, once life was back to normal for us, we decided to start trying for a little Freeland junior. After a few months of trying for a baby we realised it wasn't going to be as easy as we thought, so we booked an appointment with the doctor. At that point the doctor wasn't really worried about the length of time we had been trying because in the grand scheme of things it hadn't been too long, but for me those eight months were agony. Just waiting month after month to see if we were lucky was becoming really painful and disappointing, but we kept trying. And then it happened. It looked like I was finally pregnant! I can tell you I was on cloud nine, and jumping all over the place with joy. I hadn't had a pregnancy test at that point but all the signs were pointing in the right direction, so the next step was to get it confirmed by the doctor. Sadly though, two days before I was due to see the doctor I had to call him in as it looked like I was losing the baby. 'Well Mrs Freeland, it very much looks like you are pregnant, but I'm afraid it also looks like you're miscarrying.' His words devastated me. This should have been one of the happiest days in our lives; instead it became one of our saddest, as unfortunately the doctor was right, I did lose the baby.

I'm sure many of you reading this will understand only too well the devastation we felt, and the overwhelming roller coaster of emotions it created. Even though I was only in the early stages of pregnancy and didn't really have the time to get used to being pregnant, it took a long time for me to get over it.

After a few months we decided to try again and each month we would hope and pray that this was the month we were going to be lucky, but this pattern of trying, hoping and praying just went on month after month after month. And although we tried hard not to make it our focus it was becoming increasingly hard not to, and we were just in the process of looking at all the options we had open to us.

At the same time BP had decided to post Keith down to Dorset. Keith and I were over the moon because he had always wanted to be posted there. As with all our moves with BP it was a mad rush for us to start house hunting, find what we wanted and move within six to eight weeks. Not the easiest of tasks but as we proved time and time again it was possible.

We loved Dorset and settled in very quickly, and we were only a couple of hours drive away from Keith's parents, which was relatively close compared to when we were living in

Scotland. Very often we used to drive up to see them just for the day, and enjoy a Sunday roast with them and then drive back. It was great, and it very quickly became part of our routine. But things changed one Sunday morning when our phone rang with news that no one ever wants to hear. Sadly Keith's father, Al, had died of a heart attack outside their home while pumping up a tyre on his van. He was a wonderful man, and a great loss to all of the family. Now up until that point my connection with spirit had been a bit spasmodic mainly because of all that had happened in Aberdeen with my health, and also trying for a baby, so to be honest the last thing I would have been able to concentrate on was whether spirit were around me or not. But all of a sudden I was very aware of spirit once more, and it felt good.

From the very week of Al's passing and his funeral, I was able to feel him around us regularly, but at the same time I couldn't help but think that a lot of this was because time had stood still for Keith's mum and she was struggling to come to terms with her loss. It got to the point where we couldn't touch anything that he had left in a certain place, not even an umbrella. I can remember staying there and it was raining heavily when I needed to walk into the local town. I asked Mum if I could use the umbrella, but the answer was no because she didn't want me to move it from where Al had last placed it. So in some ways Mum was creating a sense of Al being around us, which happens so often when someone has lost their loved ones and is struggling to come to terms with their loved ones passing so they turn their home into a shrine. Of course, you have the other side of the coin also, as in that it would be easier for Al to come through and let us know he was around us because of the shrine that had been built up around his belongings. So I wasn't sure what was going on here at first, but as time went on I knew that Al was definitely letting me know that he was around.

In the beginning Keith and I would stay with his mum very frequently, and I could guarantee that I would be woken up by the presence of Al standing beside our bed. I couldn't see him, but I felt him there. I can even remember on an overnight stay when Keith wasn't with me, I even asked if I could change the room I was sleeping in, hoping and praying that Al wouldn't disturb me in a different room, but guess what? He did, and in the end I was so fed up with it that when Al visited me again, I sat up in bed and told him to go away because I wanted to sleep. I did share this on odd occasions with Keith, but I played it down because I didn't want to upset anyone in the family, especially not Keith's mum who was struggling with the loss of her husband. But it was getting to me.

My frustration was getting stronger and stronger. I so wanted something else to happen other than sense spirit around me. Why were they only visiting me but not giving me any messages that I could pass on? Why do they only let me know they are there? These are only some of the questions that I kept asking myself, and yet still no answers, just a lot of confusion and a strong feeling of being useless because I couldn't seem to get past this barrier of not being able to communicate with them.

And then at roughly the same time as all of this going on I had a visit from Keith's grandmother in spirit. This time not only could I feel, hear and see her, I was also having a chat with her. It is one of my most precious moments and a wonderful memory because not only did I know she was with me, I was getting a message from her. But the strangest thing was that when we were communicating together she was so proud to show me through her home, which is where Keith was brought up until he was 12 years old. In those days most of the time in England families lived with the grandparents. Keith's gran took me through her home and showed me what it looked like, the position of the furniture, even where Keith and his family slept. It was amazing and I was so grateful for this chat with her because it re-instilled that somehow, someway I could communicate with spirit, all I had to do was learn. Easier said than done when you don't know where to go!

Anyway, a few months had passed, and I hadn't really thought much more about what happened, until one night there was a programme on the television, and although I wasn't actually looking at the TV screen, and wasn't really taking any notice of the programme that was on, I heard a voice of a lady speaking and she sounded just like Keith's gran. I immediately looked at Keith and said, 'She talks just like your nan used to.' Keith looked at me amazed and asked me how I knew that because she had died way before I ever came into his life. I explained what had happened a few months earlier, and I can remember so vividly the stunned look on his face. I'm not sure what he made of it all at that time, but he must have been pretty spooked by it all because he phoned his mum to tell her. He never really expressed whether or not he believed that I had connected with his gran, maybe to him it was a dream, I really don't know, but what he couldn't do was deny the accuracy of the things that I had told him as it was great evidence that she had given me that night, bless her.

You know what's really funny here is that as I write this I realise that if I had allowed myself to look further afield for a spiritual church I could have had the support I needed to develop further and be with like minded people, but at the time I didn't know that the spiritual churches existed. I always thought all churches were connected to religions, which is something I didn't want to get involved with. The other thing that my upbringing and society had led me to believe was that if there was an order that wasn't connected to religion I should be very wary, as back in those days they were seen as a cult and that was a pretty frightening thought. How strange were people's beliefs then?

So by this time although I knew I had the ability to connect and communicate with spirit, all be it on a basic level, I very often found myself questioning it. Were my experiences real? Were they all dreams? When I think back now, I had put myself through such a hard time. I had completely beaten down my confidence and was questioning everything, when deep down I knew the answers to my questions, and should never have doubted it. I realise now that what I was trying to do was make myself 'normal' because I didn't fit the mould of what society expected.

I wouldn't allow my abilities to be a natural part of me; the part of me that I should cherish, honour and be very grateful for being given these abilities. As I do now. No, I saw these abilities as something that separated me from everyone else, that made me different, something to shun, and all because at the end of the day I had a huge fear of being judged. (Oh boy, was that a biggie for me!) All I can say now is thank goodness spirit were so patient with me.

All too often we allow all that we believe about ourselves and all that we do to be affected by the judgement of others. If it's one thing I've learnt in my 51 years of life it's that many of the worries that we have really do come from embarrassment, shame and fear of not fitting the mould that others want us to fit into, and although now I don't really allow that to get to me anymore (although at times it still happens), I still remember that awful feeling when I've gone against what others want. Now, I try to live each day with the principle that I don't have to fit into anyone's mould to be myself. Life's too short for that, and life is for living not for worrying about others.

If people cannot accept us for who we are, and what we believe in, then perhaps they're not really meant to share this lifetime with us.

When I think about what outdated beliefs get instilled in us from childhood, I have to ask myself is it any wonder there is so much depression, anxiety, heart attacks, strokes etc. happening in this world? We are a human body that soaks up all that we're taught, and if we've had negative and outdated beliefs instilled in us from a young age, then we're going to perceive life and all it has to offer from a very negative place, full of shame and painful experiences, and it can be very hard for us to change all of this, but it is possible. I'm living proof. Mind you, don't get me wrong, this isn't necessarily coming from our parents, although there are many cases where it has. No it's not always the parents that create all of the problems with their beliefs, it's also society, and again we're back to fitting in, and fitting the bill. Something that now makes me so angry because for many years I really believed that I had to live the way everyone else wanted me to. But that meant sacrifices and closing down that part of me that kept me connected with spirit, and all that was beyond our comprehension.

So in between looking after Keith's mum as best we could, trying to work with all that was happening with spirit and dealing with the frustrations I had around that, we still weren't having any luck with conceiving a baby, and this was really starting to get to me because over the years we had tried every option that was available to us, but still no luck. In the end we realised that perhaps the only avenue left open for us was to adopt, which now seemed to be the way forward.

When we first applied to adopt we were still living in Dorset, but sadly we were rejected due to my past health records, which we could understand and respected. We were told however, not to give up; it was just a question of letting a bit more time elapse since my breakdown before we would be considered. However a couple of years later whilst still living in Dorset we re-applied and to our amazement we were approved to be placed on the list for assessment. It was our first victory and it felt good. We knew we had a long way to go, but we were going to give it all we had. But then, as was predictable really for BP, they decided it was time for us to move again as there was a post back in Scotland that needed Keith's expertise. So out came the packing cases once again. This time our move was to the central belt of Scotland. After a few months of settling in and getting to know the area and people etc. we decided to apply for adoption in our regional area.

As we once again started our journey of adopting I was inwardly worried about whether or not my past medical history and my breakdown would have any bearing on it, and although I know we had jumped our first hurdle down in Dorset, every area is different and even if it was a very long time ago I couldn't help but wonder if it would have any effect. But all seemed to be going well at first, and once we were assigned our social worker and explained my concerns she didn't really think it would be a problem. By this time eight years had lapsed and I hadn't had a re-occurrence which was in my favour. So, all excited, we were ready for the next stage of our journey.

The process of adoption was by no means an easy task, and neither should it be, but the fact that we had a lovely social worker who had a lot of faith in us as prospective parents helped tremendously. Yes there are a lot of questions, reports and visits from social workers but both Keith and I understood this was a necessary part of the process. I can't remember exactly, but I think this first part of the process went on for about a year before we had to go in front of the board to finally be approved as prospective parents. And as we were approaching that day I was excited but nervous at the same time. We were so close now, so close to our dream becoming real. Our social worker had reassured us time and time again that everything was going to be OK and that she couldn't see why there would be any hiccups. But I had that gut feel again. That feeling inside when I just knew that something would throw a spanner in the works, but I just put it down to nerves, and put it to the back of my mind.

While we were waiting outside there was another couple there who we had met through the group meetings that we had to attend as part of the process, and we had become quite friendly with that were due to go in before us, and within minutes of us arriving it was their turn. All the while they were in there I was praying and hoping that they would be lucky, and after about 25 minutes they came out with big smiles beaming from ear to ear. I was so chuffed for them as their dream was finally coming true. Now it was our turn.

As I heard our names being called my stomach did at least twelve somersaults. I remember as we entered thinking how big the room was and how few people were there. As we sat down the chairman of the board, who was sitting opposite us introduced himself. For the purpose of this book I've called him Richard Brooke. Even though he had only just introduced himself, I felt his tone was abrupt, and not even a smile as he spoke to us. We were aware that there seemed to be a lack of panel members present, and at that point didn't quite know what to make of it. What happened next was beyond belief and although I had previously had a strong gut hunch about this meeting, I didn't expect what was coming. As Mr Brooke started talking at us, (no that's not a spelling mistake!), it was becoming more and more clear that there were so few people in the room because the full panel members were not present. He then proceeded to tell us that there was a recommendation for rejection of our application. What? How? There hadn't been a panel meeting at this point, well at least not to our knowledge because for that to happen we would not only be informed of such a meeting, but we should also be invited to attend, so if this had taken place it was totally against procedure and therefore should be null and void. Well, according to Mr Brooke this meeting had taken place. He then went on to tell us that our reports had been read by all members but it was evident in the things he was stating as 'not in the report' he hadn't read it, and when we tried to draw his attention that the answers to any queries he had were in the report he would not let us finish speaking and was totally contradicting himself with the things he was saying.

The report consisted of strong recommendations not only from doctors, their own social workers and our long term friends that we be approved for adoption, but according to Mr Brooke, these recommendations were not there. There were so many flaws in everything he was saying and doing and as we tried to talk to him to re-affirm that all the answers he needed were there for him to see he wasn't having any of it, and at one point told me to 'Stop being defensive.'

From beginning to end this meeting was against all procedures. For a start in a case where there has been a health issue as I had, there has to be a medical advisor present, but there wasn't. There should always be an adoption and fostering agent from an external agency present, but guess what? There wasn't one present! What the bloody hell was going on here? We couldn't understand why all this had happened, especially after all the reassurances we had had from our social workers! As much as we asked this man to look at page such and such for answers to a query he claimed he had, the more he ignored our request and carried on with his personal attack. Yes, it was a personal attack, an attack that had happened without any provocation. After Mr Brooke had decided the meeting was over, I had to be supported out of the room by Keith and my social worker. We were devastated, but Keith was trying to stay so strong for me because he could see just how it had affected me, and our poor social worker was just as shocked as we were. The only thing I wanted to do at this point was go home and lick my wounds.

Keith and I both felt at this stage that there was another agenda with this man, although God only knows what. But this Mr Brooke had met his match and if he thought that this would knock me off my perch and send me into a downward spiral of depression and become a quivering wreck he had another thing coming. We were going to fight this with every ounce of energy we had. Now my devastation had turned to anger. How dare this man treat us this way! If he had legitimate reasons, fair enough; if the procedure had been adhered to properly and then our application was turned down, as upset as we would have been, at least we would have felt like we were treated fairly. But to do this in such a hurtful and aggressive way, disregarding all procedure, let alone the feelings of Keith and I as he lay into us was just so wrong, and we couldn't help but wonder if there were any other couples that had received this kind of treatment from him.

What a nightmare this became. For the next three months, our life became one battle after another. Each day brought either us sending a letter out to the authorities, or us receiving a letter with some more bad news, or some more questions needing answering. It was exhausting, and there were times when it would have been easier to just give in and give up the fight, but then that would be allowing a man like that to win.

What was really interesting through all of this was that we had so much support from many social workers that we had met who were encouraging us to continue 'to fight'. It also came to light that apparently, and I have this from a very good source, Mr Brooke didn't like me, didn't believe in adoption (and here he is doing this job) and also we had discovered that he had an issue with our main social worker, Rose, and many believed that the day we were rejected was because he was out to discredit her as apparently there was an issue going on between the two of them at the time. So it appeared that we got caught up in the crossfire of the battle between them. I have to state here though that this was what we were told, not what we knew as fact and I'm definitely not claiming it to be fact, just what we were told, but it all made sense at the time. One of the things I was starting to realise about Mr Brookes was that he appeared to be a man that held a grudge, as we were going to find out later in the fight to become parents.

Anyway, back to what I was telling you. After a few months and a lot of heartbreaking days, we won our battle when we were told that we were going to be given another hearing date to apply to become adopted parents. Naturally we were really excited, but also absolutely petrified that we would be given the same kind of treatment, and all the reassurances in the world wasn't going to change that fear after all we had been through. We knew that Brooke wouldn't be part of the panel, which was a weight off our minds, but this time we weren't going to count our chickens before they hatched regardless of whether he was part of the panel or not. On the way to the meeting my stomach was once again doing somersaults, but this time I was prepared for the worse. I certainly wasn't going to go through that kind of humiliation again. This time we had made up our minds, that if there were signs of this meeting heading in the same direction as the last one, then we would just get up walk out. Once was bad enough, and we certainly wasn't going to go through that again.

OMG! What a difference! There was a full panel, the chairman was such a lovely man, the medical advisor was there to give his assessment, and in general it was such a different experience. And we were approved as adoptive parents for up to four children. At last, we were prospective parents! We didn't walk out of that room that day, we floated out. We really were on cloud nine.

It wasn't too long before our social worker informed us of two little girls that were being placed for adoption, and they thought we had the qualities these two little mites needed. Naturally we jumped at this chance, and were really excited about the prospect of becoming their parents. So all the forms were filled in, all the i's were dotted and the t's were crossed for us to hopefully be approved. Now, at this point we thought the only spanner that could be thrown in the works was if another set of perspective parents were identified, which would mean competition. That sounds awful but that's how it feels, but at the end of the day we understood if we didn't succeed then obviously the other couples strengths fitted the two children the best. At the end of the day it's about the children, not us adults. At this point though there were no other couples involved, so things were looking good, and we really believed we had left the past behind us with all the crap we had faced to become parents.

Hmm, how wrong were we! In our case, we believe the other spanner that could be thrown in the works was in the form of a Mr Richard Brooke. As I said, we were pursuing two sisters and all seemed to be going very well. We had met their social workers, and their foster parents and things were going great; the children's social worker had even given us photographs of the girls to keep. Everyone seemed keen and eager for us to become their parents. But just days before we were due to go in front of the panel we received a phone call informing us there was another couple applying to adopt the children as well. As you can imagine, we didn't feel great about this, and we were also curious as to how all of a sudden there was another couple involved, and once again this wasn't totally in accordance with their procedure to bring another couple into the picture so close to the hearing. But we would have to suck it and see what happens. Yes, you have probably guessed it, we weren't successful in our application. Once again, my gut was saying something wasn't right here, but proving it was another thing. However, we did send a letter telling the social care department of our concerns that to bring another couple into the picture so close to the hearing wasn't totally in accordance with their procedure, and how disappointed we were. However, this was not a complaint, it was just us being concerned that other couples don't go through the same experience.

So after our knock back it was time to look forward again, and hopefully the next time we tried we would be lucky. When one afternoon out of the blue I received a phone call from Brooke informing us the Social Services department who were dealing with the children's case had been in touch with them about our 'recent complaint' and Brooke, a lady called Sharon Pratt who was more senior than Brooke and their legal advisor wanted to meet with us the next day. 'I'll get back to you because I have to speak to my husband first,' I replied slightly shocked and confused.

Keith and I were worried about this new turn of events, so we phoned our social worker who didn't have any knowledge about what was going on but was of the opinion that something big was happening. When Keith phoned Brooke back to tell him we would be there for the meeting, he also told Brooke that we would be bringing a lawyer. At this point Brooke reassured us that 'this wasn't necessary.' Not knowing what to do for the best we decided that we wouldn't take a lawyer, but we would have a friend on hand just in case we needed a witness.

When we arrived for the meeting the next day Brooke and the legal advisor were waiting there to greet us, but not Sharon Pratt, the Director of Social Services as he had said in our phone call, and when we asked why she wasn't present he immediately got defensive and told us, ' I never said she would be here.' In my books that was lie number one. He then went on to tell us that the head of the Social Services department who were in charge of the children's case were very concerned about the 'allegations' we had made, and our 'reaction' to what had happened. What allegations? We hadn't made any 'allegations', all we had done was to inform them of our concerns about the way the other couple had been brought in so close to a panel hearing, which isn't adhering to their procedure, and was very upsetting for us. All we wanted to do was highlight what it's like to receive such a blow that all of a sudden another couple had been identified as possible parents also, and so close to the panel hearing. Especially when you think we had met the children's social workers, their foster parents, visited the area they lived in, got to know their likes and dislikes, and had been given a photograph of these little mites. We really felt like we knew them. But no way did we make any 'allegations'. We just wanted to make sure no other couples went through this heartbreak.

Brooke wasn't having any of it when we kept explaining that it wasn't a complaint, and in the end we asked for Sharon Pratt to attend this meeting as he had promised in the hope she would calm things down. At first he refused, but in the end he went off to fetch her. When she walked in the room I could see by her face that she wasn't a happy bunny. She immediately went on the defensive by saying that she was present when Brooke made the call to me the day before, and 'He did not say I would be attending.' Her attitude was as aggressive as Brooke's as she told us, 'I believe you made an allegation, Mr Brooke believes you made an allegation, and the director of Social Services looking after the children's case believe you made an allegation, so therefore you made an allegation.'

We had obviously stirred up something which these two were not very happy about. The meeting went so bad that I made a phone call to our friend that we had standing by to get herself down there straight away as we needed her. After about 10 minutes of having a slanging match with Pinky and Perky as I would sometimes call them, their phone rang and Pratt answered it and said 'No, not yet.' Keith and I guessed that our friend was waiting outside, but guess what, she wasn't allowed in the meeting. When we finally got past the who said what and who did what bit, we were informed that our case was being investigated and that any matching us up to children as parents was to be 'put on hold for the moment'. The next thing we knew there was going to be a meeting held to have us de-registered as prospective parents in our area.

This was getting bloody ridiculous. Every time we jumped over one hurdle there was another one waiting for us. Keith and I were starting to feel if we stayed with our regional area and fought the case even if we were to win we would always have these problems because of Brooke and knowing that he didn't like us we were always going to feel like we were up against it. So after a few disgruntled letters going back and forth about this situation we decided to resign as prospective parents and try with another agency in a different area; maybe, just maybe we would stand a chance. The laugh of all this was that even though we resigned we found out that they still held a panel meeting and had us deregistered. What a waste of bloody money! We had resigned for goodness sake. But just because we had resigned didn't mean to say we were going to let this go. Not bloody likely! We were going to do our best to bring all of this to light, even though we knew it may hamper our chances of being taken on by another agency, we wanted to make sure nobody else went through what we experienced, and we weren't the only ones suffering as a result of all that had happened. Our poor social worker Rose was now on sick leave for anxiety issues as a result of the treatment she had received by Mr Brooke and this case actually did go to a tribunal citing our case. It was quite funny really because we became known as Mr and Mrs X in the newspapers when the story was printed.

So the fight continued, and each week we would learn something new of what Brooke had said or done, never being able to open our mouth and say anything directly to him because of fear we would get the lovely people who were supporting us like this in trouble. No, we just had to keep on fighting but make sure we kept others out of it.

So through all we tried to get on with life as normal. Not an easy task I can tell you, but even though this was one of the most painful times in our life, we weren't going to lay down and let it beat us, in fact we had already started talking with adoption agencies in other areas about the possibility and they seemed quite keen, but the one thing we had hanging over our head was the de-registration. We were concerned that it wouldn't be seen as we resigned due to the treatment we received, but that we were de-registered. But we were still going to give it another go regardless.

I suppose there must have been times when I would question all that was happening and whether we going to get any further. But to be honest I don't really remember those times, all I can remember thinking is that we had got to keep on going. And then one morning my phone rang. I was busy hoovering so I asked my niece who was staying with us at the time to answer it for me. After a couple of seconds she came running into the room. 'It's that woman, Sharon Pratt,' she whispered.

'What? No, it can't be,' I said as I was walking towards the phone to take the call.

'Hello, Mrs Freeland, it's Sharon Pratt here.'

'What do you want?' I replied abruptly.

'I was wondering if you, your husband and myself could have a meeting to discuss your case.'

'What would be the point? We're no longer on your agency, and you have in the past made your views pretty clear.'

But when she said, 'I would like us to get together to see if we can discuss you and your husband perhaps re-applying to be perspective parents again,' my jaw hit the ground in disbelief and I couldn't help but wonder what this woman was up to. After all, she had been as instrumental in de-registering us as Brooke had been.

'Let me get this clear, is this a meeting where you actually want to discuss us moving forward or do you want to just sit there and hurl abuse at us the way you have in previous meetings? And is it only you we would be meeting or is it you and Brooke?'

'Let me reassure you, Mr Brooke won't be here, it will be just us three.'

Still not quite trusting her I hesitantly told her I would have to speak to Keith first and then get back to her.

Keith was as shocked as me, and as much as we didn't trust this woman we both felt we had to go ahead with the meeting, whatever she was up to.

So the meeting was set up for that night. 'Now if there's tea and biscuits on the table as we arrive, we know we're alright, and she's not going to treat us like aliens,' I jokingly said to Keith as we arrived at her office. And as we walked in the room what was the first thing I noticed? Tea and biscuits on the table. Oh, this woman was definitely licking butt, but why?

Ms Pratt informed us that she believed we were owed explanations and that we were victims of process and malpractice, and she promptly went on give many reasons as to why it all went wrong, and why she couldn't intervene before now. One of the main reasons being that we shouldn't have reacted the way we did! When I heard that it took me all my strength to keep my mouth shut because what I took from what she was saying was that we should have just taken being spoken to like that and allow ourselves to be treated in the way we were by Brooke, and keep stum! Never in a million years! If we had have stayed quiet, that was giving up, lying down and dancing to their tune, which would have resulted in our dreams dying forever. Ha, I should coco! Especially when you think of the aggressive behaviour we received from Brooke and also from Ms Pratt. However, at this stage I wasn't going to get into another argument with the woman. I just wanted to hear what she had to say now.

All of a sudden we were getting apologies for everything, and a recognition of all that we had been put through, and now Ms Pratt wanted the decision to de-register us overturned and very quickly at that! She started to talk about taking our past reports that were used in the second panel hearing when we were approved as they were still valid and combining them with a new report that would have to be made with a new social worker etc. which would be used if we appealed, and if we did she would make sure all queries a panel may have would be explained by her. And she gave us her assurance that she would 'see to it that we would not suffer any further'.

Naturally I so wanted to trust this woman and go ahead, but one of my worries was whether or not Brooke was going to be involved in all this, but Ms Pratt also reassured us that Brooke was out of the picture. What a turn up for the books! Why the sudden turn around? And why was this woman bending over backwards to make sure we were reassessed? God only knew, and I don't think we ever really got to the bottom of it, but we do have our own version as to why, but that's all it is, our own version. But it didn't matter. If this woman was prepared to help us become registered again then what did it really matter as long as it was all above board? And it really did make sense to stay with the region that we had originally worked with because it would mean that if we were successful, then we wouldn't have the de-registration hanging over our heads the way we would with other regions. So we hesitantly went ahead with the appeal, and I have to say it was hesitantly because we had got so used to taking three steps forward and five steps back when it came to trying to adopt, so why would this be any different? But it was! Before we knew where we were our application was seriously being considered for re-registration.

Just imagine our joy when we heard that we had been successful and the decision to de-register us was overturned. We were so happy, cautious but happy. We felt as though we did have Ms Pratt on our side all be it for reasons best known to herself. Once again we were in talks about the possibility of adopting, and now we didn't have any clouds hanging over our heads, and we needn't have worried about it all being above board, because it was. Ms Pratt had finally stuck to her word! I'm not sure what Brooke thought of it, but I do remember a meeting after we had been re-instated where Brooke had to be present and his attitude towards us was so different. He was full of smiles, full of chat and so pleasant, although I did notice his body language looking uncomfortable when he and I had direct eye contact with each other. I know it's a bit naughty but I did get pleasure out of seeing him looking uncomfortable at times.

Now that we had been re-approved things started to happen relatively quickly. We had gone from not being able to do anything right, to not being able to do anything wrong and getting all the support we needed to pursue two children in need of a family. It was really strange because everything about them felt so right and the more I heard about them the more I knew they were meant to be for us. Even our new social worker agreed that these two little mites seemed to be such a good match. We were frightened to let ourselves believe it, but it started to look as though our dreams really were about to come true by way of a lovely little nine year old boy and a beautiful little eight year old girl. Every step we took towards the day of the panel the more my feelings were becoming maternal towards them, and even though we still had a few hurdles to jump, I just knew that these were our kids. All we had to do now was wait for it all to go to the panel for approval.

As you can imagine we were so nervous when the day finally dawned when our application went in front of the panel for approval to adopt these two lovely little mites and although I knew deep down we were going to be lucky, I didn't want to count my chickens before they hatched. After all we had been let down before, so there was a part of me that was prepared for the worst just in case it didn't go in our favour. So I couldn't believe it when we were told we had been successful with our application and we were now the proud parents of Jamie and Katie. I can remember so clearly everyone hugging Keith and myself and congratulating us, and I wanted to say thank you but I was totally speechless. For the first time in my life I couldn't speak. We did it! We made our dream happen, and I couldn't say a bloody word! I was just so overwhelmed with joy. We finally had a family; we were complete.

Naturally there were challenges, and sometimes it felt like we were getting it wrong a lot of the time, but these two little mites that came into our life created chaos and probably caused a few grey hairs but were the best thing that ever happened to us. They are our children and we've never seen them in any other light, and you know what, I wouldn't change them for the world. In fact I would go so far as to say now I wouldn't change the course of our history, even if trying for a family was heartbreaking at times. It was meant that be that we became the parents of Jamie and Katie, and that on its own is so rewarding.

And through all this, spirit as always was with me and never let me down. They were there to guide me through one of our toughest times, and they always found a way to get a message to me that would give me hope, strength and courage to carry on. Sometimes the messages would come from them directly, and other times it would be via someone else. Like the time a friend of mine was having a medium coming to her house to give readings, and asked me if I would like to come. Naturally I jumped at the chance. 'My love I've got your husband's grandfather here who he called Father...' were the first words he spoke to me and I had barely parked my backside into the chair, 'and he's telling you that you will have your children, a boy and a girl,' he continued. He then went on to give me some great evidence along with another message from my real father. I came out of that reading feeling so high and spirit had given me so much hope that day. At that point in my life I was at a stage where I was losing all faith and doubting everything, but after that I hung onto those words until that wonderful day came when our dream finally came true.

When I reflect back now I can see just how good I got at picking myself up and starting all over again. Life still had to carry on, and I learned not to let anything get me down for too long. After all, if we don't swim we sink, and I sure as hell wasn't going to do that. After all, I had a future to look forward to, especially after the messages I had received and my gut hunch was telling me that no matter how tough things seemed at times, we were going to have our children. So until then I would need to pick myself up and keep on keeping on and go with the flow.

I've always believed that we have two paths that we can take in life. The first represents being true to ourselves and trusting our instincts, joining in the flow of life. It always sounds much easier when it's written down than when we're actually going through it. However right this path may be for us, doesn't mean to say we won't have hurdles to jump, because life was never meant to be smooth whatever path we take, but it does mean that our inner strengths, beliefs and sense of knowing become much stronger as we develop further, and with an open heart.

The second is different. It is the path where we're going against the flow of life, going against our instincts and in some cases allowing our heart and fears to rule our head and the actions we take as a result, making any hurdle we have to jump harder than it needs to be. Our confidence and self esteem also takes a hell of a battering, which leaves us very vulnerable and taints our view of life, people, and ourselves. Either way we end up where we're meant to be, but the first path will have strengthened us and opened our hearts to so much more. Whereas the second path leaves us feeling bedraggled, with so much more that we have to learn. I wonder how many of us can relate to the second path, because I believe at some stage we've all taken the wrong path and had to realise there's an easier way to living and getting to where we want to go. Remember, we can change paths at any time and start walking the one that's right for us.

Chapter 3

ALL CHANGE

Keith's job was such that he would be posted to different locations every three to four years, which meant we were on the move quite regularly. I can't say I didn't enjoy the experience of living in different areas of the UK every few years, although it did mean that we would leave our friends behind, but I'm a firm believer that true friends will always work out a way to keep in touch with each other, and there are many friends that we're still in touch with today from all the different places we lived in.

So now it was 1988 and we were on the move to Dorset. From the moment we arrived I felt like I was home. We were truly blessed with great neighbours and before long we also became great friends and I'm so pleased to say that we still are today. I immediately felt so much happier even if we were still trying desperately for children, for some unknown reason I started to come out of my shell very quickly. I was becoming more and more confident in every way. I even opened up to my friend Fran about my experiences with spirit, maybe not everything at that point, but I did share some of my experiences from childhood and some of the later ones also. It turned out that Fran's belief's in spirit were just as strong as mine, and we spent many a happy hour discussing this, and the knowing we felt within us that there is life after death. It was a great feeling to be able to share this with someone else, and I was also opening up to Keith more about my beliefs. To be honest I wish more than anything that this was something I had done from the very beginning, but I didn't trust myself with what was happening, so it was difficult for me to trust anyone else with it.

So I was becoming braver in every aspect, I had started to learn to speak up for myself, and also for the first time I had started to feel free to share my beliefs with others about spirit, but also about other things as well, and do you know what, for the first time in my life I wasn't ashamed of my beliefs. Now, I hadn't fully bloomed in this area, but the buds within me were opening up and I was starting to learn how to be me, and my inner strength was getting stronger and stronger.

The funny thing was though, that through all the growing that I was doing, and all the changes I was making, I had stopped yearning for any further support for my mediumship. I can see now that the main reason for this was that I didn't see my connection with spirit as mediumship. It was just something that happened every so often and I never for one minute saw myself developing my abilities as a medium. To me a medium was someone who was so gifted, so spiritual, so inspiring, and so not in my league. After all, who was I? But I enjoyed the connections I was getting and being able to share them with the important people around me.

As time went by the visits from spirit continued, I can't say they got more frequent, but now instead of being frustrated by not really being able to take it any further and forever wanting more from them, now I was just so glad they were with me, and I was so honoured to feel their presence. But as I have said from time to time the visits from spirit could get much stronger than just being able to sense them, it was more of a bloody wakeup call reminding me of how powerful they are when they want our attention. And again I was just about to have another one of these experiences.

When my dear friend Mavis and I went to France for four days with the twinning association of our town, we were lucky enough to be staying in a beautiful remote 120 year old country farmhouse. All sounded so idyllic until I got there. From the moment we arrived I knew there were spirit around me, in particular a female. When we settled in we were shown our bedrooms, and as soon as I walked into it I knew this lady was with me, watching my every move. I knew she was connected to the house, and I also felt that she wasn't impressed with me coming into her space. She appeared to be a strict, foreboding lady who would have liked to have been in control. She was very much like a school teacher. You would only speak when you were being spoken to.

On the first night when I went to bed, for the first time ever I was afraid, but I didn't know why. This lady's presence was so strong that I actually put my head under the covers. (What a wimp I was!) This was something I hadn't ever done before. I felt ridiculous but I didn't know what else to do with the strength this lady in spirit had. I knew it wasn't a residential haunting because she was very aware of me, and a couple of times she stood over me in a taunting way, just reminding me she was there.

In the end I got so tired and so frustrated that I sat up and asked her what she wanted, and guess what? She didn't reply, she just kept making me feel uncomfortable. Or at least I thought it was her making me feel this way. Because of my ignorance at that time I wondered if she could understand me at all. After all, I was in France and I couldn't speak the language. Oh how ridiculous I was back then, but I didn't understand at the time that there are no language barriers between spirit and us as we connect and communicate through our vibrations and energy, so they can understand and communicate with us and vice versa and I have proved this time and time again when giving readings in Tenerife, which is where we live six months of the year.

Mind you, thankfully I am learning to speak the language which really helps when relaying the messages from spirit to their loved ones. I have a wonderful friend Sonia who is also my translator when I need her and I don't know what I would do without her to be honest. Anyway this lady in spirit would insist on being around me, could understand me very well and was frustrating the hell out of me. All night long there were footsteps around me in my room, and I could also hear footsteps outside in the hallway and the rustle of a long skirt brushing against the floor with each footstep, I wasn't sure who was making the noise outside my room, and I sure as hell wasn't going to get up to find out because I had too much going on inside my room. Needless to say I didn't get much sleep that night.

When I went down for breakfast the following morning I asked Mavis how she slept, and if she heard anything going on outside her room last night. Mavis's room was opposite mine, so I was sure she had heard it. To my surprise she had slept like a log and didn't hear a thing. I knew what I had experienced was real, so I decided to try and find out more without going into too much detail of my experiences as I didn't want to freak out our hostess. So I asked about the history of the place and also whether or not my bedroom had ever been anything other than a bedroom. I found out that my room used to be the nursery and at one time going way back they had a children's nanny. This was the lady I was connecting with, I just knew it was. All that I had picked up with this lady in spirit fitted with what our hostess was telling me. I was so grateful that I could relate to what I was being told, but she was scaring me a bit because she didn't want me there and she was making that very clear. I was dreading going to bed the next night, mainly because I had already created a fear inside of me about what was going to happen. (We humans are great at creating fears out of something we don't even understand!)

Well I was right. As soon as I walked into the room to get ready for bed, she was there, waiting, and I immediately started feeling very intimidated by her presence, and lying down in that bed again was quite a daunting thought. For some unknown reason I felt more vulnerable that way. What was she going to do tonight I wondered? To be honest I had built all this out of all proportion. I really believed that she was going to harm me, which is something that my later experiences would teach me can't happen. Spirit can't hurt us if we don't allow our fear to build up. However, at the time what I did know for sure was that she didn't want me there. And as exciting as all this was I wasn't at all sure if I wanted to be there with two nights of no sleep and knowing there was a spirit in my room that didn't like me.

Yet again I sensed her in the room, hovering around me. Yes, there were footsteps again both in my room and also outside along the hallway at different times. I found myself hiding under the covers again, but it was more to try and ignore what was going on and try and get some sleep rather than because I was scared. Now I was getting annoyed because I didn't understand whether she just wanted to intimidate me, or was there something else she wanted from me? And in the end I got to the point where I sat up and told her to go away in a very firm voice. Did she listen? No! The taps, bangs and footsteps went on all night, but I had gone beyond wanting to know why she was there, so I just lay there and let it all happen around me, hoping that eventually she would just go away. Ha, if only! But the biggest laugh I had through this though was that I even tried putting the light on in the hope she would go away, which I now think is hilarious because that's not going to stop spirit if they really want us to know they're there, but it certainly made me feel better.

Once again when I went down for breakfast I told Mavis what happened, but as usual she hadn't heard or seen a thing. Oh how I envied the fact that she had been able to have two good night's sleep.

It was now the last day of our visit and I remember thinking great, we've only got one more night left. Our hosts were marvellous and had decided to have a barbecue for us and we were joined by some of their friends. It was a beautiful day, the weather was hot as it was in June or July time, and their friends were lovely. We all had some great laughs and the language barrier didn't get in our way. But for me all I could think about as the afternoon turned into the evening was whether or not she, the spirit, was going to be paying me a visit later that night. I was dreading it, and yet at the same time I so wanted her to be there.

As I hesitantly went to bed that evening I noticed that things were calmer, and there was no sign of my new friend, or at least I couldn't sense her. The room was lovely and quiet and kind of peaceful, but not totally. So now I had the chance to have a good night's sleep before travelling the next day, but the funny thing was, as tired as I was I couldn't sleep because I was waiting for her to return, which sadly, she didn't do.

On the way back to England I was reflecting on what had happened in those few days, and the different experiences I had there. It was frustrating and exciting all at once, and this time it had gone on for days, not just for a few moments. Oh yeah I was tired but what a great experience! This time I was very clear about what I was picking up from this lady in spirit. Her description, personality and although she didn't actually say anything to me, we were definitely communicating with each other, she communicated through my clairsentience that she didn't want me there. Yep, I certainly got that message. When I was back home I think I shared this with everyone that would listen. Another big change for me from the previous times. You know though, the greatest thing was that I finally didn't care if someone thought I was off my rocker, I just wanted to share my experiences which was a huge change for me, and it felt so good.

So life carried on, and I carried on with it, just doing my daily routines, but this time things didn't go back to being the 'normal' that I knew! My little experiences were becoming more frequent, and with each connection with spirit my belief and confidence was quietly growing within. Although I have to say I didn't see what the future held for me at that point, in more ways than one. And talking of seeing the future, my connection with spirit wasn't the only thing that was becoming stronger, but also my psychic abilities as well, which, at the time I wasn't aware that my psychic abilities were all part and parcel of my development. And yes there is a difference. Let me just briefly explain this to you.

Our psychic abilities is when we go beyond our five senses and tap into our sixth sense, our intuition, our gut, and when we tap into this we receive a wealth of information and receive guidance about situations that we are going through.

The problem is that many a time we tend to ignore our intuition and let society or others dictate which path we should take. And yet, if we were to listen to it in every situation it can change not only our perspective and outlook but it can change every aspect of our life.

Each of us has a unique energy field surrounding our physical body. Our 'Auric Field' that has different layers of energetic vibrations which, not only surrounds our physical body, but is also connected to our seven main chakras. Each layer of our aura and each chakra integrate with each other all of the time, and are connected to our physical, mental, emotional, and spiritual state. Our aura also holds every memory we have in this life time, along with all the stresses, strains, challenges and moods.

So when we're picking up psychic information from another person, we are actually reading their aura. Should we want to we can all develop our abilities to a level where we can give psychic readings, but be warned, it takes time and practice, and of course permission from those you wish to read. When we tune in to another person's aura we become receptive to information about their past, present and perhaps we can even get a little glimpse of their future. Believe it or not we don't only pick up on names of those who are close to your sitter, but we can also pick up on their loved ones who have passed over, which is why so many people get so confused between a psychic reading and a mediumistic reading.

When reading psychically for a sitter, although we may be able to pick up on a loved one that has passed, our information and evidence will be limited because we are only reading from the person's aura, not connecting with spirit, but there are some who get confused and believe that because they have received names, and the relationship between the sitter and their loved ones in spirit and other little snippets of information that they are connecting with a particular spirit. I'm afraid this isn't the case. It's very important when deciding to take the path of a medium that you choose a training that focuses on showing the difference and teaching you how to connect psychically and connect mediumistically.

Back to my story! So now my psychic abilities were going from strength to strength, I was listening to my intuition far more, and I stopped letting my heart rule my head, and went more with what felt right. I also became so sensitive to the emotions and feelings of those around me, and in some situations I was even able to pick up on the outcome of a present situation either for myself or for others if we didn't follow a certain path. I didn't go looking for this info, it just happened, and there were times I wished it hadn't because not all of the outcomes had a happy ending. I have to say that although it seemed freaky at the time, there was nothing magical or mystical about this, all that had happened was as I started to open up and accept that I had the ability to work with spirit, I became more confident in myself and all that was possible, which allowed me to develop my abilities even further both as a psychic and also as a medium. I didn't know it at the time the strengthening of my abilities was standing me in good stead for what lay ahead in my future years.

I had started to perceive life in a very different way, and my husband Keith helped me with this also, as he has always had great intuitive abilities and has proved to be very psychic on many different occasions.

I do want to make it clear though, I am not a predictor. That's not my bag. A little bit of guidance and a bit of information on what path to take is good enough for me and I'm more than happy to leave predicting the future to the fortune tellers out there.

At this stage of life I was quite happy to accept that the visits from spirit were about as good as it got. Although, as much as I loved to share my experiences with close friends and family I wasn't prepared for it to go any further than that. I had heard the way mediums were treated and spoken about by others and I knew I just wasn't strong enough to be judged by others in a negative way, and trust me that's exactly what it was like back then. Thankfully now things are getting better and people are opening up far more, but the human race have a long way to go before they reach that final acceptance that life after death does exist, but hopefully now we're on the first rung of the ladder of starting to realise that there's far more to this universe than the physical world alone.

This is where I really missed having the support I needed to develop a greater understanding of what was happening to me. I had so many questions I wanted answered. I was curious to know why it was happening to me. After all, I was just me, nothing special and I didn't come from a long family line of mediums, at least not that I was aware of, so why?

I never really had any faith in myself, not on any level, and like I said before, I didn't think I was medium material. I wouldn't be that lucky. I had always been quite a nervous person and from as far back as I can remember my confidence and self esteem had been so very low, and being judged, shamed or rejected because of my mediumship would seriously have knocked the stuffing out of me. No, I just wasn't ready, and I can remember thinking at the time that life was difficult enough without me adding more anxieties to it. So I put my questions and frustrations on the back burner for now.

However, my belief in spirit had never weakened, and my experiences in France had only strengthened it. In fact it had gone beyond believing to a sense of knowing that when our loved ones pass over, their spirit still lives on, and are very capable of connecting with us and proving their continual existence and growth through the tiniest of details that they give in messages. I had only then just started to appreciate all of this as the most wonderful and amazing thing ever, and when spirit gives that proof either directly to a person or through a medium and a one to one reading gives such a boost. I know the effect it has on me when I receive messages from family and friends in the spirit world. For me, there's nothing that can beat it.

Like the time my real father James came through saying how sorry he was, and could I find it in my heart to forgive him. Now, there's no way in a million years that conversation would have taken place had he still been alive, well at least not at that time anyway. We were both stubborn and pig headed, and to ask such a thing of each other, would have been giving in, and that was never going to happen. We would have quite happily just gone on not wanting to speak to each other, so the rift, anger and bitterness would have got deeper and stronger. Thankfully though, I had done a lot of growing since those days and although it was hard, the time had come for me to move on, never forget but forgive. Yes it felt emotional and difficult to hear all the things that he should have said while he was still here, but to realise deep down he had a conscience was quite heart warming. This was a side to him that I never saw. He knew he had wronged my mum and us three kids, and that day I could feel him with me, genuinely regretting all he had done and it was refreshing to know that he hadn't escaped his actions by passing over. He still had to deal with the consequences, even though he was in spirit. Since that time he has come through many times and nearly always at a time when I've needed a bit of support or guidance, which has helped me to make decisions at difficult times in my life. In a strange sort of way I've had more of a relationship with him since he passed over than I ever did when he was on this earth.

But it's important to remember that it's not only family and friends that give us support; our spirit guides and teachers are always on hand to give us the advice, support and encouragement we need in every aspect of life, and I have always found they've gone through amazing lengths to ensure not only that they get their message across, but also to keep us on the right track. All we have to do is reach out and ask for them to be near and allow them to be part of our life, and I have to say that for me, I have always found their guidance and support so comforting as I walk along my spiritual path. They gave me the understanding I needed to learn how to let go and live instead of hanging onto old wounds that were crushing me inside, so by the time James came through I was ready to forgive and move on. I felt as though I could finally close that chapter in my life, and start a new one. Of course what I didn't realise was that the new chapter was going to take every ounce of energy and support that spirit cold give me and my family to survive all that was ahead.

Chapter 4

FAREWELL MY LOVELY LU-LU

As I said in the previous chapter, only when we lose someone close to us, can we truly appreciate the value and the power of spirit. Receiving a message either directly from spirit or through a medium amidst our grief really is priceless, as I was about to find out.

It was December 2001 when my family's world was absolutely turned upside down, and life was never going to be the same again. On December 30th in the early hours of the morning we had a phone call to say that my sister's husband Chris had been found dead in their home. He was only 45 years old.

'Ang, Ang, wake up, Sue's on the phone; Chris is dead!' I could hear Keith saying to me as I came out of a beautiful slumber.

'What? No. it can't be! Chris dead?' I replied as I started to come around, not quite being able to take in what I had just heard, but I could see by Keith's face I had heard him correctly, Chris had passed. The next question was to find out how.

'Mummy's being questioned by the police,' my niece Sue blurted out.

What the heck! Why? This was going from bad to worse! Thankfully my aunt was staying with us at the time so we could leave the kids with her while we went over to my other niece Michelle as she was in the thick of dealing with it all at this point. By the time we got there my sister Louise had been released. Lu-Lu, as I called my sister, was in bits and wasn't making a lot of sense as to what had happened, or why the police had questioned her. According to my sister, the night before they had a row and apparently she hit him with the hoover causing him to fall to the floor where he lay because he couldn't get up, and off she goes to bed. I must point out at the time of the row they had both been drinking heavily. On the way home my head was reeling from it all and I was really worried because I had a nasty gut feel. 'You don't think my sister could be done for this do you?' I asked Keith.

He paused for a moment and then replied, 'I doubt it.' But my gut was saying something very different. But for the moment I had a more important problem lingering. How the hell was I going to tell my mum and dad this kind of news? Lu-Lu wasn't in any fit state to tell them, neither were the girls for that matter. Like all of us, Mum couldn't take the news in and passed me over to my dad, which was a bit of a blessing because I could at least tell Dad straight what my concerns were, whereas with Mum I wanted to protect her and save her from all this. The next day was New Years Eve. A time to reflect on the past and look to the future, but for our family none of that was important right now. The only things that mattered now were coming to terms with Chris's death and making sure my sister and the girls were OK. Although my nieces were adults and mums themselves they were going to need a lot of support to get through this.

For the sake of our children Keith and I tried to keep the day as normal as possible, that was until we received another phone call from our niece Sue telling us 'Mummy's been arrested on suspicion of murder. Michelle is at Romford police station giving them a statement, I've got the police coming to me, and Jake (Michelle's then partner) has been taken to yet another police station to be questioned!'

I immediately went into a blind panic, not knowing what to do. My sister arrested for murder? No! Our nieces being questioned? Why? This can't be happening! It was like a script out of a soap opera. Only it wasn't a soap opera, sadly it was real, as real as it could get, about as serious as it could get. Or so I thought. I can't remember if Keith was at work for a few hours or if he was out somewhere but I remember phoning him asking him to get home straight away.

We decided the best thing was to go to Romford Police Station where our niece Michelle was being questioned. There was nothing we could do for my sister at this stage, our other niece had her partner with her and Jake could look after himself, but Michelle was in a terrible state and even if we couldn't be in the room with her, at least we were outside waiting for her. Yep, that's where we needed to go.

'I'm Mrs Freeland and I've come to pick up our niece Michelle,' I stated as I got to the police counter, and within minutes the door was being opened by the man who had been questioning her and thankfully she was right behind him. He seemed a nice guy and wasn't intimidating in any way.

'Mrs Freeland, you're the sister of Louise – yes?' he asked and confirmed in the same breath.

'Yes,' I replied hesitantly wondering what was coming next.

He continued to tell me 'We need to interview you as well. We can do this here and now or we can come around to your home first thing tomorrow morning; which would you prefer?'

I wasn't expecting that one! I opted for the next morning at home, but why all this questioning of the family? None of us were there at the time of Chris's death. In fact I hadn't seen my sister for a few weeks, so what could I say that would be so important? Well, tomorrow would tell, but meanwhile I had another phone call to make to Mum giving her an update, and there was no way I could keep this from her.

Once again Mum passed me onto Dad.

'Don't you go telling anyone about this. I don't want anyone to know.' he shouted down the phone angrily. Dad always raised his voice when he was annoyed even if it wasn't you he was annoyed with. I was starting to feel angry with the statement that he had just made. Did it really matter who knew, or what they thought? That wasn't priority at this stage and I didn't need that pressure of feeling like I'd got to lie because it didn't sit comfortably with Dad, and it was by no means going to be an easy task because family and friends were already starting to ask questions, and now I felt I needed to lie to please dad. Nice!

The next morning the two policemen that were dealing with Lu-Lu's case arrived right on time, and after settling ourselves down with a cup of tea and their tape machine was switched on the questioning started, for two solid hours. What was my relationship like with my sister? Did she have a temper? What was her relationship like with her husband? When was the last time I spoke to her? I had to go into the 'ins and outs of a black cat's arse', as my mum used to say. By this time the penny had started to drop. They're trying to build up a profile of my sister and what she was like, from childhood to now. Never in a million years did I think I would ever be doing this, and for such bad and sad reasons. The two policemen were really nice and although they weren't interrogating or intimidating in any way, I felt like I had been dragged through a hedge backwards. And now it was time for poor Keith to be interviewed, thankfully for him though it wasn't as long as my interview. By this time my sister Lu had been released on bail 'pending further enquiries' and these enquiries went on for three long months. Because of all these 'enquiries' we couldn't even bury Chris until a good seven weeks after he passed. It was bad enough for us to think of him not being laid to rest, so I can't even begin to imagine what his close family must have felt. As a family, we stuck together like glue and we all knew if my sister did have anything to do with Chris's death it definitely wouldn't have been premeditated.

The next two and a half months were extremely difficult for myself and my family as we watched my sister struggle to come to terms with what had happened, and the acceptance that Chris was no longer around. It was such a painful time for us all, especially her two daughters. For me watching her go downhill was one of the hardest things I've ever had to see, and even as I write this now the tears still well up, a lump in my throat and the pain in my heart still so strong as I remember the turmoil she was going through. I knew deep down inside that she wasn't going to pick herself up. Oh, she was trying but the battle was getting harder and harder for her. But just as we all thought that life couldn't get any worse, that it couldn't get any more turbulent than it already was… oh, how wrong we were. It was just about to get worse, far worse.

My family and I supported my sister as best we could. We could all see her health deteriorating quickly but we all kept on going as best we could, especially for our children as it wasn't fair on them to be all doom and gloom and they needed some normality back in their life, so we all carried on regardless.

By the time all this happened we were living in Essex, as Keith was now working there. This was a blessing in disguise because my sister and her children had also moved to Essex, so at least I could be with them through their hardest times. We still owned the property in Dorset and we would often go down there for high days and holidays, so after all that had happened we decided to spend a few days there to have a break with the children as they had a weeks' holiday. I can remember us saying, 'The break will do us all good.'

There was a part of me that really wanted this break, and yet there was another part of me that wanted to stay at home just in case… and as I started to pack our suitcases the warnings got stronger. A cold shiver went down my spine, and I heard the words so clearly: 'Be prepared; something bad's going to happen.' I went so cold because I knew that whoever's voice that was, they were right.

So off we trots down to Dorset trying to grab back some time with our children and the first few days were great, although a bit tense, but on the whole the children were pretty good and we had all started to relax and enjoy our few days away. Obviously my mind was still on my sister, but I knew she was being very much supported by her children. I started to think to myself that maybe that voice I heard was my imagination, but deep down I knew that wasn't the case. Like

I always say, we always have to listen to our gut, so I just had to wait and see. It turns out I didn't have to wait for too long.

On the morning of Friday 15th March I remember waking up at 8.20 and I was freezing, absolutely freezing. I couldn't work out why as it was mid March, and although I know that March can be cold, it was never this cold. I felt like a block of ice, and no amount of jumpers was making any difference, and it didn't get better as the day went on. In fact I just kept getting colder and colder. In the late afternoon we decided to take the children out for something to eat, and even in a nice warm restaurant I was still so cold that I even ate my meal with my coat on, which is something I never do. I also had a feeling of doom hanging over me and I just couldn't shake it.

When we returned home we all got stuck into watching TV when my mobile rang. My niece Sue was at the end of the line. She only had the chance to say 'Hello,' when we got cut off. I went into a real panic because as I was trying to call her back I knew she was going to tell me something I so didn't want to hear. Bad news. That was an understatement. I'll never forget those two words my niece said to me once I got through.

'Mummy's dead.' Those words still echo in my ears today. My lovely sister had passed away. I couldn't take it in; I couldn't believe it. I can remember screaming, 'No! No! No!' so loudly as I collapsed into a chair. Poor Keith and the kids were wondering what the hell had happened. Keith had to take the phone from me to continue to talk to my niece, and the kids, bless them, ran over to my friend and neighbour Fran and asked her to come over. I was inconsolable. Nothing, but nothing had prepared me for that. Not even the gut hunches I had been having could have prepared me for that.

Lu-Lu had passed away quietly at home, and I later found out that she died at around eight in the morning, but hadn't been found until six in the evening. When I found out the time she had passed I couldn't help but wonder if my feeling like a block of ice all day and growing colder by the hour was me tuning into my sister's passing and her body going colder once spirit left it. It may sound crazy, but it did seem strange to me how I had felt all day, and what was even stranger was that as soon as I was told about my sister, the heat in my body came back immediately.

Sadly my sister had been alcohol dependant and her fragile body had finally had enough of all the abuse she had put it through over the years. For a long time she was able to keep it under control, but sadly as each year passed, the more she drank the more she lost control, until in the end she couldn't get through a day without a drink. It was heart breaking to watch a girl I loved, had grown up with and in the early years had looked up to, slowly destroy herself. She was a stunner in her day, and she knew it; and when she was a teenager there was always a boy knocking at our door wanting to take her out. Over the years I saw her go from a beautiful, confident, strong-minded, larger than life and very proud person to a skinny, dishevelled, selfish wreck. Why? God only knows, although I have my own thoughts on that one. What I do know is that my family saw my sister slowly slipping further away from us day by day and even to this day, I can't help but feel that we lost her long before she passed.

The week in between my sister's passing and her funeral is still a bit hazy. There was so much to do, and yet none of it was real to me. I just wanted to detach myself totally from the whole situation, but knew I couldn't. I can even remember when I had to phone friends and family to tell them, I would say, 'Louise has passed.' Only by calling her Louise could I detach myself from the pain. You see I very rarely called her by her proper name, to me she was Lu-Lu. Saying 'Louise' kept it all at a distance, at least until we had got through the funeral and even on the day of her funeral, nothing seemed real. Saying goodbye knowing I wasn't going to physically see her again just wasn't sinking in.

After her funeral we all started to try and pick up the pieces and try to come to terms with the two losses in less than three months. Our worlds had turned upside down but life had to go on. So I painted on a smile and pretended that I was coping with it all OK, when the truth was that I wasn't coping, I was falling apart and I couldn't accept that she had gone, and I had started to withdraw from everyone, even my poor husband and children. Oh, I could go into automatic pilot and do all the things that were necessary to meet their basic needs, but I wasn't there emotionally for them, and this went on for a while. Every night when I laid myself down to sleep I used to wish that a year would pass by very quickly so that the rawness of what I felt would be healed. When I think back now, I can't believe that I was wishing time away, especially as my children were growing too quickly anyway. I just wanted some normality back (whatever normal was). If I felt this bad, I dread to think how my mum and two nieces had felt through this time. I would have given anything to take their pain away but knew I couldn't, which made me feel really useless at the time.

The heartbreaking end to this story was that even though my sister had passed away, so effectively there was now no one to answer the charges that had been made against my sister, an inquest on Chris's death still had to be held, which Keith, my niece Michelle and myself attended. It was gruelling having to sit through that hearing, listening to all the gory details once again but it was so worthwhile because the verdict on Chris's death was 'accidental'. The truth is that only two people really know what went on that fateful night; and since his passing we had all been making up our own stories as to what went on, so hearing what was said in court helped us to finally piece it together more. My version of what happened that night is that they had an argument, which was nothing new, and it is likely that my sister did hit him, probably with the nearest thing to her which was the hoover which caused him to fall to the ground, and because he had been drinking and because of his size he was unable to get up, and as a result hypothermia set in. So it wasn't actually the blow from the hoover that caused his death, it was because he couldn't get up once he had gone down and in the eyes of the police Lulu had caused his fall, and all evidence pointed to her leaving him there instead of trying to seek help for him and ensuring that he was warm if nothing else. The consequence was when she came down the next morning, poor old Chris had passed away. Believe it or not, the actions, or lack of, led to her being arrested for manslaughter, and at the time of her passing she was out on bail while the crown prosecution decided if there was a case for her to answer to. It's just a shame Lu-Lu wasn't there to hear it for herself, but at least it gave us all the chance to finally move forward and start our grieving.

A few months had gone by and I was still struggling to come to terms with Lu-Lu's death. But you know I was so wrapped up in my grief that I hadn't even tried to call her forward to let me know she was alright, and if she was around me I certainly wasn't sensing her. I think the reason for this was because I still wasn't accepting that she was gone, and if I had sensed her around me or tried to connect with her, it would mean that I would have to accept that she was no longer physically here. I really believed at the time that accepting that she was gone would destroy me.

Until one day I was attending a course that I was on for my psychotherapy profession and was driving along listening to one of my favourite artists, Whitney Houston. I knew each track off by heart and their sequence on the album, and I was also very aware which song was on when I turned the engine off (this is very significant to what I am about to tell you).

Our tutor had decided this day that we were going to do a meditation. I can remember not being much in the mood for this but knew I had to do it. So I made myself comfortable and relaxed. I was focusing on my breathing, becoming more and more relaxed when the next thing I knew my sister was with me. I could feel her love so strong, and I could see her with my spiritual eye. It was wonderful, and she had the most profound message for me. 'You need to let me go! You're holding me in your hand not in your heart.' She also told me that she was with Chris and they were at peace. Well, I wasn't expecting that! And as I came out of the meditation I was shocked, dazed and happy all at once, and the tears were rolling down my face. I knew what had happened was not my imagination, my sister had come to me to help me let go and grieve, and by doing this it would allow her to rest in peace. This was all too much for me and I had to make my excuses to leave the class. I ran out of that building, my emotions were all over the place but I managed to compose myself enough to drive home.

As I switched the engine on Whitney Houston started to blare out again, but this time it wasn't the track that was playing when I parked, in fact it was nowhere near the track that had been playing, instead the track that was playing was a song that both my sister and I loved, *I will always love you*. This song was very significant because we had actually had a row over who the original singer was, and as usual when it came to music Lu-Lu was always right. This time though the words in the song had a whole different meaning. *If I should stay I will only be in your way, so I'll go, but I'll think of you every step of the way. But I will always love you.* As I listened to the words it almost felt like she was saying them to me. She was saying her goodbye.

I couldn't believe it, she had also let me know through a song that it was time for her to go, but most of all it was time for me to let her go. Her place was no longer with us here on the physical plane but she will always be with us in spirit. I knew exactly what that message meant, and I knew exactly why she would choose a song that already meant so much to me. You see my sister had felt as though she had been a burden for a few years before she passed because of the different challenges and health issues she had. We had many deep conversations over time about the different challenges she had and how she felt dependant in many ways. But the truth is we would sooner have her here beside us with all the issues she had, rather than have lost her when we did. I realise now that was a really selfish way of thinking about it. I may have wished her here with me, but was she actually able to cope with all that had happened and what she would have had to go through? Looking back now, I don't think so, and as she reminded me in the message, it was time for her to go, and she was at peace. As hard as that was for those of us left behind.

For the first few days after I had connected with my sister I was a bit of a wreck, very emotional and very, very tearful. I did share what happened with my family which I felt eased our pain just a bit. It was nice to know she was still around us, still hearing us when we called her name, knowing how much we missed her. But the one person I couldn't share this special experience with was my mum. I was too afraid that she wouldn't believe me, but more than anything I was more concerned with whether or not she could cope with it. Either way I wasn't going to chance it. I regret that now, I wish I had shared the blessing of what I had experienced that day, it may have made her last few years on this earth a bit more peaceful.

The message I had received from Lu had helped me to put some kind of routine back into my life, especially for the sake of the children and it was now time to come out of my shell that I had withdrawn into and slowly get back into living a life again. The problem now was that although I was making slow steps forward, I was still hanging onto the wonder of that communication with her, and for a long time after I would pray that she would come again, just for a brief while just to know that she's still there, but it wasn't to be. You see I understand now that spirit won't just come in because we want them to, there has to be a reason, not just because we're missing them, or struggling to be without them. Spirit know that's all part of the grieving process, and they know we have to learn to live without them otherwise we'll never let them go. Lu-Lu had given me all the reassurance that I needed in my message, and she told me what I had to do, so at the moment there was no other reason for her to come forward, and I was going to have to learn to live without her.

Yep, spirit are amazing, and it's only because of what that message from my sister did for me was I able to understand the power of receiving a message from those we love and lose, and how it can help us to rebuild our life. I don't think we ever really get over losing someone, but receiving a message from them in spirit helps us to come to terms and accept that they are gone, especially once we know they are OK.

Now my focus was very much on my family, especially my mum. Something inside me knew that she would never really pick herself up from losing her daughter and so often I felt guilty that I couldn't change that for her, and would you believe for a while I even felt guilty that it wasn't me that had passed instead of my sister. Crazy but true! I never in a million years thought I would feel this way and I didn't understand why I would carry such a burden as this, but I did. I used to phone my mum regularly and visit her as often as we could, which wasn't easy with two teenage children, and both Keith and myself working but we did what we could. We did talk about Lu-Lu a lot but Mum never really let me into what was going on for her. Not that she needed to because I could sense and see her sadness not only in her face but also in her energy and I found myself trying to compensate for Lu-Lu not being there anymore, and of course Mum was starting to put more pressure on me to visit more frequently. I know she didn't mean to put that pressure on me, and I know it was only natural that when you lose one of your children you would want to see and speak to your other two children as often as you could, but it was hard, and understanding the reasons as to why she was like this didn't make it any easier for us.

It was always lovely to go over and visit Mum but I was never really comfortable with the energy in the house. Oh I know Mum and Dad could be volatile at times, which would make the energy sting a bit, but it was more than that. I always felt as though there was a presence around us. I did ask Mum about the history of the house, but to her knowledge nobody had died there, and nothing bad had really happened there, so I couldn't understand why I felt the way I did. Let's put it this way, I never felt truly welcome there, and it got that bad that there was many a night when I woke up needing to go to the loo but I was too afraid to so I waited until the morning. I can't say I used to hear things go bump in the night, but I very often felt a male spirit gentleman around us. This gentleman neither said nor did anything, apart from to allow me to sense his presence. It was like a warning really, a warning saying that I needed to behave, naturally I respected his space and behave I did.

I was curious, especially about her living room which is where I felt most uncomfortable, and a particular corner of the room. I used to be drawn to this corner and whenever I stood there I could feel such a strong energy pulling me back and at times I would lose my balance. I was freaked and intrigued at the same time. There was more to this house than we were aware of, and although a few years later we unearthed more of what was happening there, we never really got to the bottom of it.

Now, I'm not really that superstitious but I often wondered about the lack of luck that Mum and Dad had there. Not long after buying their house and moving in they went through some financial difficulties, Dad was also diagnosed with cancer, but thankfully went into remission. There always seemed to be one thing after another, but they loved their new home and Dad especially loved the land it was on, so I suppose that was the most important thing. Of course what I realised very soon after starting to develop my abilities was that Mum and Dad's land had a negative energy, and by this I don't mean spirit, I mean the residue of what was left behind from all those that had previously walked on that land and let's not forget all that had happened there. Oh, how I wish I had known how to cleanse negative energies from homes, land etc. back then. I would have definitely got my smudge sticks out.

We can't always link paranormal activity solely to the house that it's happening in because so often it's connected to the land, and yes we can cleanse homes and lands of stagnant or negative residues that has clung onto them. Of course many a time we may have to go further and actually use a rescue kit to release a spirit that has attached itself either to someone's home or the land it's on for whatever reason. But I do have to point out that it's no good going in with the attitude that you're stronger and more powerful than spirit, and you're definitely going to get rid of whoever is there because that will get you nowhere. They were there first, and providing they're not harming anyone why shouldn't they stay? After all, how would you feel if someone came into a home where a member of your family in spirit may still walk and try to overpower them and their rights. As you have probably guessed I feel very strongly about this and when we're called into an investigation I never go there with the intention that I'm going to free the house of any spirits that may reside there. That would be pretty big headed of me to think I have that right, and I tactfully try to explain this to those who live there, and let me tell you if spirit don't want to go, they won't, no matter what you do. The important thing here is that you need to know what you're doing because if you don't, you can make it far worse.

When doing lost souls work it's important to remember that these spirits need healing and help, not someone going in all gun-ho with an arrogant attitude. We're not there to prove how strong we are, we're there to 'hear their story' and to help them to make that transition back to their spiritual home and back in the fold of their loved ones who are waiting to be reunited with them. And it is so wonderful when this healing and transition takes place, and of course the added bonus to this is that when we help to heal another, be it spirit or someone here in the physical world, then healing takes place within us. That's the best kind of reward you could ever get.

Anyway back to what I was telling you. Mum was finding her own way of dealing with her loss, as was I, but I think Mum's way of dealing with it was by shutting down and never really talking about it. Mum was a bit like that, she never really spoke about her parents either. They had both been in spirit for a number of years along with some of her brothers and sisters. Yep, Mum had suffered a lot of losses in her lifetime, and I suppose she learned that was the way to deal with it, and

I had learnt to get used to her being this way but it did make me feel shut out a lot of the time. So often I wanted to talk about it, I wanted to share my experiences, but most of all I wanted to support Mum as much as I could but couldn't because she had locked it away.

They say out of every negative there is a positive, well for my own peace of mind I had to look for a positive with all of this. If I couldn't find the reason for why we lost Lu-Lu, then I had to find something that could be seen as a legacy that she gave us to carry on, and as crazy as this sounds I found her legacy. I started to see that through my sister's passing she had given me the greatest gift, and that was the gift of life. Because she was so young when she passed it made me realise how fragile we are in life. One minute we are here physically and the next minute we are in spirit. That scared me so much and made me realise just how much of life, and of those around us that we take for granted. We get up every morning and for many of us we just think it's the same old, same old, but it's not. Every morning when we wake up we have chances, opportunities and a day ahead of sharing the love that's around us. Oh yes, we may know deep down how precious those we love are to us, but because of the stresses and strains of life, the aiming towards goals and dreams and how we're going to find happiness, so often we take it all for granted. We look for what we want in life without really appreciating what we already have.

Now don't get me wrong, we shouldn't spend every moment of every day saying thank you, but it's so valuable to all of us if we spend just a brief moment of every day thanking God (who or whatever God means to you) for who and what we have, and when we do, we automatically feel the happiness that so often we don't realise we already have. Don't take any days for granted my friends, even if it feels the same as yesterday because it isn't. With each new day comes a new chapter of life. Oops, I've just realised that I've got on my soap box! As you can probably tell, I feel so strongly about never taking things for granted and I have my sister to thank for that. Lu-Lu had definitely given me the gift of life when she passed, and she has helped me to unlock and realise I needed to develop very much as a person before anything else. And in a strange way the door that needed to be unlocked within me happened because of my loss, and the way I saw it, and still do, is that if someone gives you a gift like that, then you don't let them down, and I wasn't going to let her down.

Maybe that was the wrong reason to decide to make the changes I wanted, but it was the right one for me, and there was also something inside of me telling me that I was being guided and helped into making my choices at that time. I honestly believe Lu-Lu played a part in helping me to move forward in life, in every aspect. I know that may sound silly but it's true. I'm convinced she wanted me to challenge my beliefs and recognise what was right for me and not for everyone else, and I also believe she was hell bent on making sure I start to live my life incorporating all that's important for me no matter what. This task wasn't going to be easy as I felt so much fear at the thought of being more open and honest with others about my beliefs, experiences and my values. I spent half my time worrying about what they may think of me, but you know sometimes we've just got to have faith and trust in our guides, in spirit and in all those who guide us, and I decided now this time had come.

Wow, what an eye opener this journey was going to be! I really thought I had unearthed and dealt with a lot of my past hurts, feelings, emotions and experiences when I was training as a psychotherapist, but boy oh boy I hadn't even began! I realised I was only on the first layer but I was determined, no matter what, that I was going to do what it takes to open up and really start to understand how I tick. What I didn't know at this time was that the more I worked with my true self, the closer I became to spirit. The more we're true to ourselves, and learn to let go of all that closes us down and find an inner peace, the more we can hear the gentle whispers of sprit calling and guiding us and there's nothing quite as wonderful as hearing our name being called by those we love and our guides.

The first part of my journey was going to have many hurdles and stumbling blocks, and in a lot of cases my stumbling blocks were of my own making, particularly as I didn't trust very well. I didn't trust myself, others or life with my most inner thoughts and feelings, and the true reality is that I didn't know how to. I had put such a strong guard up to protect myself because of all the hurts disappointments and pain that I had had over the years. But I do want to say here though that the one person that has never let me down or disappointed me is my lovely husband Keith, even though it did take me a long time to put my trust and faith in him, not because of anything he was doing, it was more about me and not allowing anyone near me, so it took him a long time to chip away at the brick wall I had built around myself and break it down. My word, he had some patience and staying power. A lot of people would have given up, but thankfully not Keith. He was and still is always there for me, and I can honestly say that he has never let me down, never disappointed me, and has played a huge part in allowing me to develop and be true to myself, and has always been by my side no matter what it took.

The new path I had ventured to take was strange, enlightening and testing as I tried to work out who I was and what I stood for. To look back at what we've believed for so long and realise that perhaps those beliefs don't sit comfortably with who we are, and maybe, just maybe those who taught us were still living in the Victorian era with their beliefs and values is quite difficult. Now I know that sounds harsh, but for me it was true. Half of what my parents believed about life, religion, people etc. didn't fit for me. At first I felt as though I was betraying them by going against all they stood for, but I also realised that half the reasons I got myself into so many scrapes and rows that I had when I was young was because there was always something inside of me that was fighting against what I saw as antiquated, and wrong attitudes towards life. This must have been so hard for them as well, as in their eyes I stood for all that they were against and didn't believe in. Well, as you can imagine this created a whole heap of dysfunctional dynamics between me and my parents. I laugh now because I can remember Mum getting so wound up when I used to rebel against her and voice my opinions and she would say 'You would argue with a saint.' How right she was, and even when I was older, married and had children, me and Mum used to go at each other like the two hot heads we were. Oh how I miss those times! They all seemed pretty serious then, but as I look back now, I think they were funny, and I realise now that there were better ways to deal with things other than to go at it hammer and tongs just trying to prove who was right. One thing I must say though is that although Mum and I were very often on a different wave length and annoyed and angry with each other, the love we had for each other was strong, and that never faded, even if we didn't always show it. I'm just sorry I gave her such a hard time.

Oh, here I go rambling again, but all of this became important and helped hugely with my personal growth. Starting to look within to find that peace that we all long for isn't easy, and although it's just a change of attitude that starts the ball rolling for your self-development, it's important to know that you will come up against issues that are going to create an inner conflict, certainly at the beginning anyway. In many cases you are going to spend a lot of time fighting against what you were taught to believe in, and you are going to feel as though you're up against it for a lot of the time, but you just have to trust and hang on in there. And for any of you budding mediums out there, knowing yourself is a very vital part of the process as you move and work towards being an ambassador for spirit.

I can guarantee that you do find that inner peace, and a greater awareness that not only helps your perception of life to shift but it brings you closer to spirit.

Thank you Lu-Lu for opening the door to all that would change my life, and for the better.

Chapter 5

BINGO!

At around about the same time of all of the changes within me taking place, society was also changing their views about the paranormal and there was a sudden interest in things 'that go bump' in the night, and now there were many paranormal programmes flooding the TV. Now think what you will of these programmes, whether you think they're fake or not, in my opinion they were very instrumental in opening some doors that was seen as 'mystical', 'out there', and 'crazy'. These programmes gave us permission to think outside our box, and as their success shows, people were looking for something, be it ghosts or explanations, or trying to disprove spirit were around us. Whatever the reason, they were looking for something. Everyone was watching them, including me and for the first time ever, working with spirit was starting to be accepted.

This was great; there were mediums and psychic studios popping up all over the place. All of a sudden it started to be the 'in thing' to believe and talk about it openly. What a change! All of a sudden my world had opened up and I had gone from not knowing where to turn and accepting this was as far as I could go, to being spoilt for choice. For the first time ever not only did I have choices but I started to realise that there were places I could go like Spiritual Churches and meet like-minded people.

At this point I hadn't really considered signing up to a workshop or psychic development course. To be honest I always thought they would be expensive, so for a while I was just happy watching my programmes and thinking about how good it was that these programmes proved I wasn't so freaky after all. Secretly though I was wishing that I could go on an investigation, just to experience it. Well Keith must have read my mind because he decided to surprise me by booking us on one. As you can imagine I was over the moon! I bet he didn't think for one moment though where this investigation would lead on to, as it was the turning point for me. I wonder if he's lived to regret that surprise.

So we went along and to be honest I thought I was going to be scared witless. The investigation was taking place in a huge mansion in London. As we were approaching it I got such a strong sense of sadness, all these emotions came up and I didn't have a clue why. I didn't know the history to this place, but I was soon going to get an idea! I was so nervous that night, but my nerves were more about how many people would be attending and what they were like.

The paranormal team that was hosting the evening spent quite a lot of time with us before the investigation, teaching us techniques to raise our energy and heighten our senses, which is something that I believe is important when you want to work psychically and mediumistically and there are many ways we can do this. Anyway when we were walking around with the team's medium, I was picking up many things psychically, but one of the things that really shook me was the amount of anger I felt when I touched the banister on the staircase. I had never felt anger like it, and it got worse with every step we took as we headed upstairs. As we got to the top of the stairs we all stopped while our team leader and medium was talking. I looked around at everyone and I could see on their faces that most of them were experiencing something. Not necessarily the same as me because we all pick up different things through different senses. We all have a more dominant sense, i.e. some people are visual so they will see pictures when thinking about something, or some may be auditory because their hearing will be more predominant in general, and before making any decision something has to sound good for them. Now, the trick when doing paranormal investigation is to strengthen all of your senses in order not to miss a thing, once again there are many different tools and techniques that will help you do this, and there are a lot of great books out there that gives some great tips and advice.

But getting back to the investigation, we were all standing on this landing sharing what was happening for us, when all of a sudden Keith piped up and said, ' I just want to throw myself over that banister.' I couldn't believe my ears! Keith had never ever spoken like that before so for a brief moment it freaked me, but of course it wasn't Keith that was feeling like that, it was what he was picking up from the residue that had been left behind. Phew!

We continued the walk around, going from room to room being encouraged to work psychically, which was great and I was loving every minute of it. But as we walked into one of the main rooms things changed from working psychically to working mediumistically as I sensed a gentleman spirit around me, and to my amazement I could see him standing there through my spiritual eye. This wasn't psychically, it was mediumistically. He was in a WW1 army uniform. I could see him as clear as day and as the team leader started explaining how the building was used during the war I found myself saying 'But it wasn't the Second World War, it was the first,' and I also gave him the name of the gentleman and his connection to the property. He confirmed I was absolutely right. I have to admit I was rather pleased with myself, not only because I gave good evidence, but more because, for the first time ever I spoke up about what I was getting. As the evening wore on the same happened again when we were in the kitchen. I was connecting with a lovely female spirit and was sharing it with the group. With each area I went into I was getting more and more. It was great.

After our walk around we headed into the dining room to hold a séance. I was enjoying the activity and I could really feel spirit around us wanting to work with us, but then to my great surprise the medium looked at me and said, 'I have a friend of yours here and she has a message for you.' He described a very dear friend I had lost the year before.

I'll never forget that message because it meant nothing to me at the time, but ten days later it would be very significant. She told me I would feel like I was over my head in paperwork and wouldn't know where to turn, but not to worry I'd get through it. I couldn't think what this could be linked to, so to be honest I shrugged it off and got on with what we were doing.

That night was amazing. We had a lot of activity and by the time we got to the last vigil it got really lively with noises. People were being pushed, we had white noise on the radio and spirit were so good and responded to anything I asked of them. You can probably tell by now, I had found my confidence and it was me that was doing the asking because the group felt I was getting results.

I was so tired for the next few days, but I was also on a high, and although Keith was pleased for me that so much had happened, and a lot of it around me, he was worried that I didn't know what I was doing. After all this was a first for me and I was lucky, but what if something had happened? What if the activity had got out of hand? How would I deal with it all then? He was right of course, so I decided now was finally the time for me to do something about it all and thankfully with the blessings of Keith. He was behind me all the way. So my next step was to check out what was on offer and sign up, but I didn't want to rush this because being on the right course was important, but there was another reason why I wasn't in a hurry, and that was because I was so nervous about making the next step. To be honest I didn't think I had it in me to make the grade! But just as I was about to take that next step it all had to go on the back burner again as life took another sad turn. My mum passed away.

I had always dreaded this day. I know me and Mum had our differences and our relationship could be, well, let's just say it could be volatile at times, but I adored her. We were just too alike, both head strong. But two days before Mum passed I had the most wonderful conversation with my mum that many don't get the opportunity to have. It was deep and very meaningful, and I feel so blessed that I had that opportunity.

I had just got home from work when the phone rang and to my surprise my mum was on the other end of the line. Now, I say this was a surprise because Mum never phoned me. She always waited for me to phone her, but she wanted to say thank you for her birthday present I had sent her. We started talking about her age, by the way she was 82 years old, where time had gone and what an achievement it was to be 82 years old. Then when the subject hit on dying, Mum admitted to me that she was scared. I never liked Mum mentioning her passing and I would always say, 'Mother, you're not allowed to die because I don't do black.' This used to frustrate the hell out of her, which used to tickle me, but this time it was different, I listened and felt so emotional as she spoke about it because I could hear her fear and I realised for the first time just how vulnerable Mum felt because of her age. It was also important to her that I was clear about her wishes for her funeral etc.

Anyway, once we got that all out of the way we moved on to lighter subjects. I can remember feeling so close to her through this call, and when I got off the phone I remember feeling really good. I have to say that I had the same experience with my sister just days before she passed. Both the conversations with my sister and my mum were beautiful, in-depth and honest, and the memory of these calls still keeps me feeling so close to them both even now. I knew that Mum hadn't been feeling great recently, but she seemed to be making a good recovery. Poor Mum had had a rough couple of years because she had two falls and on each occasion she had broken a hip and as a result she had to have hip replacements in each hip. It was difficult enough for her to recover from the first, but to do it again and have to have a second replacement really knocked the stuffing out of her, but slowly and surely she was getting over it.

So when the phone rang on the Sunday morning I just couldn't believe what I was hearing. I had always refused to accept that Mum was going to pass some day, and now it was here, she'd gone. Naturally the first thing we needed to do was fly over to Ireland to be with Dad, so Keith, our niece Michelle and myself flew out that day and our children were going to follow a few days later. I can remember sitting on the plane waiting to take off and I couldn't help but wonder how me and my Dad would be together now that Mum was gone. You see Dad and I had a very up and down relationship, but I did see him as my dad, and I was going to be there for him no matter what.

As soon as I walked in Dad stood up and hugged me, which was so special to me because I hadn't really ever had a hug from him before. I could see that everything was going to be alright between us, and nothing was going to change that, well certainly at that point anyway.

After Dad and I had a good heart to heart and shed a few tears I decided to get ready for bed, and being the good girl that I am I always have a cleansing routine that I go through every night, but I had forgotten to bring a hair band to put my hair back when doing it, so I went into the bathroom where Mum kept all her hair grips, clips etc. On top of the box that Mum used to keep all this stuff in there was a side comb of hers so I picked it up to see what was underneath it. As I was ploughing through all of her stuff, I became aware of Mum standing by my side. Her energy was so strong and I knew she was letting me know that she was there. To feel her next to me on the very day that she passed was so overwhelming, but also so comforting. Of course I didn't realise then that me holding Mum's side comb in my hand may well have strengthened her link with me. I spent a lot of time in that bathroom that night feeling her presence and telling her how much I love her, begging her to come back. I knew she was hearing me because I could feel her energy almost embracing me. It was an amazing experience, but God, I would have given anything at that point to have her back with me and for us to be having a good old argument. Then it would all be alright. But at least she let me know that she was going to be around us supporting and guiding us through all that we had to face. I also have to thank our family over in Ireland as they were absolutely wonderful, and being as I didn't have a clue how to go about arranging a funeral in Ireland, I wouldn't have known where to turn without them.

As with every sad situation there will always be something that will bring a little chuckle or a smile to your face, and the night before the funeral certainly brought a smile to mine. When we made all the arrangements for the funeral we agreed with the undertaker that only immediate family could visit Mum in the chapel of rest from Monday to the Wednesday, and as of Wednesday evening she would be open for family and friends and all who wanted to pay their last respects. My niece and I were to be there from 5 p.m. onwards whilst Keith would pick our children up from the airport. So, off we go thinking we would be there for about an hour. Well, I had never seen so many people coming in to pay their respects, even the postman and her doctor, but what was more surprising was that they would come into the chapel, pay their respects to Mum and have a chat with my niece and myself, and then off they would go to the kitchen, which was the room next to the chapel and make a cup of tea, and come back in with their tea and biscuits. I was standing next to Mum's coffin at one point when my cousin brought me over a chair, a cup of tea and some biscuits, which to be honest I was so grateful for as I was starving. I couldn't believe I was sitting next to my mum who was in her coffin and I'm drinking tea and eating biscuits. I can tell you it was one of the strangest things I have ever experienced.

But you know what was so lovely was that everyone that came to pay their respects that day had a lovely memory of Mum to share that brought a smile to our faces; lovely little memories of the woman we all knew, and in some cases they showed a side to Mum I didn't really get to know. There we were standing over her chatting and sharing the times they had with her. It was lovely, a real social gathering that wasn't full of doom and gloom but of happier times and lovely little insights into a lady we all knew and loved.

The funeral was just as… er, well, let's say it was different, and I swear Mum was playing a very large part in making sure it all went the way she wanted! I can even remember when I was writing out what I was going to say when I talked about Mum at the service and I also wanted to choose some prayers that I thought she would like. As I went through her prayer book and asking her at the same time what she would like, as I wasn't sure which one to pick, I was feeling a bit tired so I decided to have a break, and put the book down on my bed and was just about to leave my room when I turned around and to my astonishment the book had opened at a prayer aptly named Safely Home, which is about returning to our spiritual home and being on the arm of Jesus (remember Mum was a Catholic and believed very strongly in Jesus). Yep, that was Mum, choosing what she wanted. I still become emotional when I hear that prayer, because it doesn't matter what our faith and beliefs are, the common theme through all faiths is that we do return to our spiritual home and once again in the arms of our loved ones. And as a medium my experiences verify for me that when we pass, we do return back into our spiritual homes once more, and are re-united with our loved ones.

Mum wanted to be cremated and taken back to England, which doesn't sound too hard a task except it's something that isn't that common where Mum comes from. So we would have to go through to Dublin for the actual cremation service, but first we wanted her to have her main service in the church that she was christened, which is also next to the little house that used to be the school that Mum and her siblings went to. So all of this was organised, the date was set and all we had to do now was to get through it.

As you can imagine, Dad was so upset about Mum, which is only natural, but his grief was doubled as their dog had passed a month before Mum passed, which devastated them because they adored their animals. So losing Mum on top was just devastating for him. And that week of the funeral all he kept saying was now that he had lost the pair of them, he had lost everything. It was so sad seeing him suffer like that and I felt so useless. Dad wasn't going to the funeral because he didn't believe in 'churches or religions', although he wanted to make sure mum had the send off that she wanted, and he left that part to me. I also think that Dad didn't want to go to the funeral because he didn't want to say goodbye to Mum which, as we all know is so hard to do.

The day came to say farewell to Mum and as we pulled up outside the church for the service I could see the people gathering but my attention was more on a beautiful little dog that was jumping up and trying to say hello to everyone. She was gorgeous. As we started to enter the church I had a quick stroke and thought no more of it and went into the church for the service. Well, half way through the service to our amazement down the aisle walks this beautiful little dog. She walked around Mum's coffin, went up to say hello to a few people and then came over and sat by my feet. I think everyone in the church was trying not to focus on her and concentrate on the service, but I can tell you it wasn't easy. After the service we had to head into Dublin for the cremation so I had a last little stroke with her and off we went. I tell you I could so easily have picked up this little beauty and taken her home with me.

I wanted to put all the flowers from Mum's funeral onto my nan's grave which is in the grounds of the church we had the service in, which meant we had to go back the next day to do this and to my surprise the little doggie was there, waiting. Dad had decided to join us that day for the ride, which was unusual for him, but some things are just meant to be because as soon as Dad and the dog clapped eyes on each other there was an immediate bond and Dad just said, 'I'm taking her home.' We managed to persuade Dad to hang on until we checked out if she was owned by anyone, after all you can't just take a dog because you want to. So Keith and I decided to knock on doors near to the church to find out. I can tell you I would have paid any price at all for my dad to have the dog.

As luck would have it, we had a result on the very first house we knocked at. The lady there told us that the dog just showed up ten days before, and that she had been looking after her but couldn't keep her permanently. So this lovely little dog was going home with us. My dad's face just lit up, it was a delight to see. Now maybe I'm reading too much into it but I'm convinced that Mum had a lot to do with this lovely little mite turning up and giving my dad a reason to live. He even named her after my mum, which for me was very strange to go around calling her by my mum's name, but it was what he wanted. Yes, I'm convinced she was making sure in her own way that we were all doing OK, and that our needs were being met.

Of course there was the other side of things that had to be taken care of as well. You know the insurances, etc. and although Dad dealt with a lot of it, Keith and I helped where we could with the paperwork, and believe me this was no easy task, especially when Mum and Dad kept cases of the stuff and not that well organised either. There was one day when feeling like I was over my head in paperwork and that it was never going to get sorted when I remembered what the medium told me on the night of the investigation. 'You're going to be up to your eyes in paperwork but don't worry you will get through it.' My dear friend in spirit was warning me that there were tough times ahead, but also letting me know that I will get through it. I found it so comforting that spirit was able to be with me and give me some support through the tough times, and you know we all get that kind of support from spirit when we need it. They're always there with us, never forget that. All the little things that happened through that sad time, all the little blessings that were given to us, were in my opinion being given to us from spirit, and they did make such a huge difference. Yes spirit guide and support us through so much, and very often we don't even realise.

I miss my mum every day, but I always know she's with me, and I very often feel and hear her around me. Thanks Mum.

Chapter 6

MY NEW JOURNEY

So once we all got over the shock and started to pick up the pieces it was time for me to make the first step on my new journey. I was still dragging my feet a bit because I was more worried about Dad, but Keith decided to take the bull by the horns and search out a good course for me that met all my needs. It sounded great and it was going to be over a period of 18 months. When the first weekend came I was excited, happy and very, very nervous as I didn't know what to expect, but at least I was moving my butt and doing what I had dreamed of for years. This first weekend of the course was being held in a beautiful little village called Pluckley in Kent, which apparently is one of the most haunted villages in England, so it had a lot to offer us. I couldn't wait.

It was brilliant and we were learning to do so much psychically and mediumistically, and for the first time ever I learned how to meditate and blend energies with spirit. I can tell you, it was a really weird experience. I immediately felt spirit around, in fact it was more than just feeling him around me, I actually felt as though someone was pressing on my face, and then I had a fit of coughing. I couldn't stop and was finding it hard to catch my breath so in the end Mark, our teacher, had to remove me from the group because I was disturbing all the rest. When we got outside I immediately stopped coughing and started to feel better. I shared with Mark about the gentleman spirit pressing on my face just before the coughing fit and he confirmed that he also saw him and agreed that my new friend was 'a little mischievous'. He also told me that the coughing was him trying to manipulate my voice box, and not to worry. I couldn't help but think how can you not worry when spirit are trying to manipulate me? In that short time I spent with spirit before he so rudely tried to kill me through coughing, I had picked up quite a lot about him. Firstly I knew he was male, I knew he was connected to the area and I could also give a rough date of when I thought he was there physically. Not bad for the few minutes I was with him.

Then came the time that I had to connect with spirit for the first time ever in front of my peers, and yes, typical me I was getting myself into such a state inside of me because I was worried that I would get it all wrong. When I look back now I see how stupid that all was, but it was the first day and I didn't want to look like the class idiot. How egotistical. Anyway whatever was going on internally I certainly wasn't going to let it show. What I didn't expect however was the emotion I would feel.

My very first connection was with a young lad of sixteen who passed over as a result of running away from bullies. I can't remember the whole story now but he was riding on his bike when he ran into a group of boys who were bullying him because they wanted his bike and they started to threaten him. In the desperation of trying to get away he fell into a river, got caught on something and drowned. Apparently his connection with Pluckley was that his grandmother had lived there. Afterwards I couldn't stop crying. I was in bits and couldn't stop the tears from rolling down my face. I can remember Mark trying to calm me down and telling me, 'It's not your emotions, it's his. You have to learn to stand back from that.' But I wasn't so sure that all of the emotions I was experiencing were because I was feeling the emotions of the young lad, after all who's not going to be emotional when you know this lovely young lad died in such a horrible way? It was all very strange.

I suppose I thought that all messages were going to be all flowery and sweet, and that all spirit that comes through would have lived a long life before passing over and that their passing was a natural one. How naive of me! Mind you it didn't deter me. I may have been naive but I was willing to learn, and there was so much I was going to have to learn but I knew from that early stage that my commitment to working with spirit was very, very strong. By the time the weekend had ended I was exhausted but I was on such a high. We even had homework to do for the next course, and anyone that knows me knows I love homework. So very different from when I was at school!

After sharing the weekend with spirit and like minded people, the next few days were really difficult for me to come back down to earth and get into the swing of normal everyday life. I was going through a whole heap of emotions which Martin warned us about, but what was really strange was the feeling that cobwebs had been swept away from my face so that I could finally see clearly, and I also felt like my ears had been cleaned out and I could finally hear properly. I know that sounds weird but it's true.

Although I eventually got back into my routine I wasn't going to let the stresses and strains of the day affect my work with spirit, and every day without fail not only did I do my homework but I would also sit and ask spirit to blend their energies with me. I was building up a relationship with them. The problem was that I was constantly willing them to come forward, and as usual they didn't let me down; I was encouraging them to be around me all the time. I was getting messages, becoming aware of friends' loved ones who had passed and I even had visits from spirit in the middle of the night. There was one occasion when I woke up and needed the loo, so I got out of bed as you do and started to make my way to the bathroom, when all of a sudden I walked into an energy field which felt so strong that I actually bounced back. Straight away I knew I realised there was a spirit standing there. I apologised to my visitor for bumping into him and continued my way to the bathroom As I was sitting on the loo it came to me what had just happened, so on the way back knowing they were still there I calmly said, 'I'm sorry, as much as I would love to chat with you, I'm too tired. Could you come back tomorrow please?' and I got back into bed. I couldn't believe I had done that, but I knew I had to start putting some boundaries in.

You see I had lost my grounding and as crazy as this sounds I was living more with spirit than I was in the physical world, and that's no good to anyone particularly if I wanted to give readings in the future. I have learned over the years that in order to be a good vessel for spirit they need us to have both our feet firmly on the ground in the physical world. They want us to live a 'normal' life and experience the things we're meant to, but if we spend most of our time trying to have both feet in the spiritual realm (which, by the way is an impossibility no matter how hard we try), we're going to end up becoming what I would call 'airy fairy'. Now my definition of 'airy fairy' is someone who wants everything to be linked to spirit, every sound, every sensation without putting the logical part of their brain into action, and let's face it, not everything is connected to the spirit world.

After a few more sessions on the course things started to go wrong and dates were being cancelled. At first we were promised new dates, but then we stopped hearing from them all together until in the end I came to the conclusion that this course wasn't going to go any further. I was gutted. I felt as though I had come so far and now I was back to square one and didn't know where to turn once more. There was no way I was going to stop working with spirit, I knew that for sure, so now I was back to browsing the internet for another course to join and to my astonishment one of the finest mediums in the UK had a psychic studio just ten minutes up the road from me. That studio was the Tony Stockwell Psychic Studio, and in my opinion he is one of the finest mediums there has ever been (pedestal or what!), and my luck got even better because they were just about to start a new course just a month later.

Naturally at first I was hesitant at what to expect, especially after what had just happened, and yes it was a very different way of teaching, but it was every bit as good. They had us learning about our senses and which is our strongest one when connecting with spirit. They also had us working with our spirit guides, helping us to bring messages through from spirit to people in the group, and doing platform work. We learned something new and something different every week but I didn't stop there, along with my weekly circle I was also attending other courses, I was reading every book about mediumship I could get my hands on, but I also wanted to be pushed even harder, so I decided that I wanted to be mentored weekly.

I couldn't get enough of working with spirit. My mentorship consisted of two full days per week working with the wonderful medium and friend Mandy Gray. She had me working so hard that I sometimes felt as though I had been turned inside out. At this point I never really had any intentions of working with the public, I just wanted to be the best vessel I could be for spirit and that was reward enough for me. I was at Tony's studio for about a year, and my mentorship was for about a year also. At times fitting all this in was so difficult because Keith and I were also working full time, bringing up the kids, although by then they were young adults, which helped a lot, and of course we were still going over to Ireland regularly to look after my dad. We also phoned him every day without fail no matter where we were because Dad wasn't coping at all well with the loss of Mum and his health was failing, but more concerning so were his moods. He was slowly sinking into a depression that nothing or no-one could bring him out of. He told me so many times that he wanted to die and be with Mum. It was heartbreaking to watch him slipping lower and lower and there was absolutely nothing I could do to help him apart from looking after his immediate needs and to let him know we were there for him, but we knew he would need more care as time went on, and we must do all that we could to support him. I still had my psychotherapy practice and although Keith had retired by this time, he had gone straight into partnership with his best friend Paul and together they built a very successful business which did entail them being away from home, but not to the degree he was when he worked for BP. So keeping this in mind Keith and I decided that we would spend three weeks working and then a week to ten days in Ireland with Dad.

As exhausting as it was, it did work well and for a while Dad did pick up, but it was short lived I'm afraid. Even though we had a lot on our plates I was determined that I was still going to find time to meditate and work with spirit, even when we were in Ireland, I always put that time aside for me and spirit. To be honest, I think it kept me sane with all that was going on in our lives. I needed to know that spirit were near me. I would very often go off on my own to work with spirit, and what was really funny was the more I worked with spirit, the more things would step up around me, and when we were staying with Dad some really freaky stuff started happening. Like the day I once again sensed the gentleman around me but because I was busy getting ready to go out I didn't acknowledge him or try to connect with him, which was a bit naughty of me. Anyway as I was starting to get changed the swivel mirror that stood on the chest of drawers started turning over so that the back of it was on show instead of the mirror. What a gentleman this spirit was! I knew without a doubt that my new friend had done this, but being typical me I wanted to prove it to myself by trying every which way I could to get the mirror to do exactly what it had just done, but there was no way it would repeat it. For me that was the verification.

Because of all the goings on in Dad's place I also spent half the time taking photos looking for orbs. For those of you who aren't sure what orbs are, they are circular light anomalies which many believe is spirit starting to form, and yes, I am one of those believers, and whenever I took a photo in Dad's although I got a lot of dust, in fact mostly dust, many times there were also orbs amongst them. A lot of shadows started forming and in general Dad's house seemed much more active. I didn't dare tell Dad because I was worried he would think I had a screw loose, but naturally I shared it all with Keith.

However, there was a turning point for Dad. He started talking of seeing a man and a young child in his bedroom and he told me that the young boy would often sit on his bed. He could describe what they looked like, what they were wearing and what they had said to him. Poor old Dad, he was starting to think he was losing his mind until I reassured him that I had seen the same man and he wasn't imagining it. Although he didn't say anything to me when I told him what I had experienced I could tell he was taking it all in. What a change in a man that had always believed once you're dead, you're dead. See, it's never too late! Now, although I had connected with the man that Dad was talking about, I hadn't sensed the little boy, but that doesn't mean to say that he wasn't popping in. The man was somehow connected to the land as he had been a farm hand many years before and was still doing his job checking all was OK and that we weren't doing anything he wouldn't approve of. He was very stern and strict and I got the impression that he didn't like strangers, neither when he was in the physical or now he had passed.

As I said before, the room I hated the most was the living room. Whenever I got near it I knew there were spirit around, just popping in and out as and when they pleased, and not all were connected to the land. It felt a bit like a free for all at times and it always made me feel uncomfortable. There was a certain corner in that room where I could feel so much energy and if I stood there I would be pulled back with a force. It was strange. At first being quite naive I thought perhaps it was a vortex/portal where spirit could come and go, but as I became more knowledgeable I wondered if the electric points that were there were creating that energy field and also the feelings within the room, but that wouldn't explain the spirits I had sensed and connected with many times. I had also spoken to a few people with far more experience than I had and they agreed with my original thoughts, oh I'm sure the electricity currents that run through the sockets in that corner were helping them to build their energy but because of my experiences there I knew it wasn't the cause. I spent many an evening there in the dark just waiting for a visit and nine times out of ten they did. I met all sorts: male, female, young, old, friendly and some not so friendly. It was a great place to stay in that respect, and as I said before there's so much more to this place than meets the eye.

All of this working with spirit was great, but it did have some drawbacks at times like when working with a client in my psychotherapy practice. One minute there was just the client and myself and the next minute there would be the client, myself and their nan, grandad, or their Auntie Gertrude with me, and as much as I wanted to share this with them, I knew it was a no-no because there are boundaries that one doesn't cross, and that was one of them. It was hard but I had to learn to keep my psychotherapy work and my spiritual work separate, which was such a shame because I'm sure if some of my clients knew they had their loved ones with them this would have given them such comfort. In truth this was becoming a bit of an issue for me as I was struggling to separate them. In some ways it felt like I was being tested by spirit to see if I would keep those boundaries in place and respect them at all costs, and yes, I did, but not without difficulty. But on the other hand it was also very rewarding watching the aura of a person growing stronger, larger and far healthier as they worked through their problems, and this was something I did share with them as I thought it was important that every positive change and improvement was recognised.

At the same time of all of this happening I had been feeling a bit under the weather for a while, but typical me I just ignored it. I was having really bad headaches, palpitations, loss of concentration and extreme tiredness, and these were only a few of the symptoms. I just put it down to the stress that was in my life at that time. I was also aware that Mum was around me a lot of the time, in fact most of the time, so I took the opportunity when I had the house to myself one Saturday afternoon and called her forward. Mum came through straight away and told me to 'Go to the doctors, I'm concerned about your health.'

Now to be honest this wasn't the kind of message that I expected to hear, and being as I saw myself as a novice I thought I had got it all wrong. I was also at the stage where I doubted every message I got, so I asked, 'If that's truly you Mum, give me a sign.' With that the doorbell rang and surprise, surprise nobody was there! So I promised I would go the following Thursday as that was going to be my easiest day.

When Thursday arrived and although I wasn't working and was at home, the day had turned out to be busier than I thought, so I didn't bother making an appointment to see the doctor. Well, the door bell kept ringing repeatedly and each time there was nobody there again. Keith thought that our bell was tuned into somebody else's along the street, but nobody would have had that amount of people knocking at the door in one morning, and it was too much of a coincidence. This went on all morning and I can remember shouting out loud to Mum, 'OK, OK, I give in. I'll go tomorrow.' Guess what? The door bell stopped ringing, which we were all so grateful for because it was doing our heads in.

So the next morning I kept my promise and went to see the doctor thinking, this is a waste of time, I'm just tired, that's all. But I was wrong. I explained to the doctor how I had been feeling for a while, but I omitted the part about Mum talking to me from spirit, otherwise he may have called for the little men to bring in the white coat! Well, let's face it, it does sound pretty 'off the wall' to say 'I'm here because my mum in spirit told me she's worried about my health'! No, I think it was better to just talk about how I felt physically. The doctor was great, he listened and examined me, but when it came to him taking my blood pressure he seemed quite concerned. He requested that I have a 24 hour monitor put on me, and I should come back the next day.

This machine was a real pain going off every few seconds and there's me trying to work with the noise of it, and my arm expanding continuously, not literally but the thing they have wrapped around your arm. It also kept me awake all night, but thankfully it was coming off the next day. When I returned to the surgery I saw the nurse to have it taken off me. I asked her if she could give me the reading, but she said that all she was able to do was say if it was high or low, it had to be the doctor that gives the actual reading. So off she goes to take a look at the reading, which is all computerised, but I was starting to get worried that she had forgotten me because she had been gone so long. When she eventually returned she told me it was very high and I had to see the doctor.

'Your blood pressure is dangerously high and you have no idea how close you have come to having a stroke or a heart attack. If you hadn't have come now you would have ended up collapsing.' You could have knocked me down with a feather when the doctor told me all this. I just didn't have a clue and the reason for that was, as usual, I was ignoring all the signs my body was giving me. A big lesson learned. Don't ignore the signs your body gives you, and of course it proves never ignore spirit either.

My mum, bless her, may not have been here physically, but she was just as determined to make sure I was OK. Once a mother always a mother, even when she's in spirit! Mum, once again you saved my bacon. Thank you so much. It's funny how things fall into place. When I look back, apart from the physical signs, there were also very strong signs that Mum was trying to warn me but not only was she warning me, she was nursing me as best she could. I can remember just before I went to the doctor I used to lie in bed and I would feel someone stroking my forehead very gently. It was wonderfully relaxing. I guessed it was Mum because I knew she was around, and all of this confirmed to me that it was her, and now I know why.

After having such a scare like that I needed to do some thinking and make a decision as to whether to carry on working the long hours I was doing or simplify my life by retiring and spending more time with Keith and the kids. Obviously I would still have to go over to Dad's but at least I wouldn't be feeling so exhausted. I loved my job but it was time to move on, although not immediately because it would take months to support my clients as they work towards an ending with our sessions. I wanted to make sure they didn't feel in the lurch. This was so important to me because so many of them had been left high and dry so many times in their life and I wasn't going to repeat the pattern and let them down.

I was sad that my work life as I knew it was coming to an end, but I could also see so many positives in it as well. First of all my mind went to how lovely it would be to spend more time with my family and then secondly I was getting excited at the prospect of being able to work more with spirit. By this time I was able to give readings but hadn't really delved too much into that, and we were attending some paranormal investigations but not too many manly because of the cost. Sometimes the cost of attending investigations was outrageous, but I won't get started on that or I'll never shut up!

So only another eight months to go and I was going to be a free woman. No more work and less stress, perfect! I had a whole heap of feelings running through me, most of them positive, but I did have some nagging thoughts about retiring and I kept wondering if I would enjoy no longer working. I kept thinking how busy I had been for so many years, how would I adapt? But as always I needn't have worried because spirit had other plans for me.

Whenever we were in Ireland and going out and about, I was always drawn to a sign that said 'WICKLOW GAOL', and had a real desire to go there. Now, I didn't know anything about this place, and I didn't want to find out until I got there because I have a policy never to research the history of a place that I might end up investigating in the future. It takes all the fun out of it and anyway I want to learn from what I pick up psychically, and also hearing the story of what those who were interned in the gaol suffered. But I have done so many investigations at the gaol now that I have a rough outline of its history.

Wicklow Gaol is situated in the heart of Wicklow Town and was built in the 1700s and was used as a prison, but also as army barracks for the English and the French. Through my connections with spirit there I know there were people hanged for different crimes including horse stealing; there were many who were only there for a short time and were lucky enough to survive the awful conditions and were released, and sadly there were those who died in there as a result of illness and diseases that swept through the prison.

Let's not forget the political prisoners who were also interned there, whose lives would have been made hell because of their beliefs, and there were also many poor prisoners who were transported from the gaol to the Americas, or New South Wales. Their journey certainly wasn't an easy one. The ships would have been overcrowded with harsh conditions to endure which sadly would have been too much for many of these poor souls to suffer and sadly led to their death before they even reached shore. I can only imagine that this kind of treatment must have not only broken them down physically, but mentally and emotionally as well. I'm not going to go too much into the sordid details of the gaols past, but I will say it is so steeped in history and most of it absolutely devastating. If you haven't been there, it's really a place I would put on your to do list. It makes a person realise just what so many suffered not only there but in other places like the gaol, and for a budding medium, let me tell you there is always a spirit around that would love to have a chat with you!

One day while talking to my cousin and mentioning it to her, she told me that she knew the manager of the gaol. Of course being a little cheeky I asked if there was any chance she could get us in there out of hours so that I could have a look around. She was an absolute star because she managed to fix it. From the moment I walked in there I was picking up on the sadness and heartache those who were imprisoned there had suffered. But I wasn't only picking up on the adults, but also on the poor innocent little children that had been imprisoned. It was absolutely heartbreaking. For me there was so much unrest and sadness seeping through the walls. As we did our walk around, we headed towards the dungeons. When we were in the isolation cell, I Immediately connected with two gentlemen that I knew had been confined down there, and I also knew that as they walked out of that cell they were walking towards their death. I could feel their fear and desperation and I don't think they were the only ones who walked that path from that cell.

At the end of the evening we were speaking with the then manager of the gaol and told him everything that I had picked up on. He knew exactly who these two gentlemen were and confirmed that they did indeed leave that cell only to be taken out and hung. Little did I realise at the time how important the gaol would become to me.

Early publicity shot at the infamous Wicklow Gaol; "one of the most haunted places in Ireland".
Picture by Peter Evers.

In action at a Wicklow Gaol public paranormal investigation. This picture made the Irish national newspapers!

Early publicity shot at the infamous Wicklow Gaol. Picture by Peter Evers.

Publicity shot taken during Keith and my time with Irish Ghosthunters. Picture by Peter Evers.

Angie Freeland Psychic Medium publicity.
Photograph by Paul Page Photography.

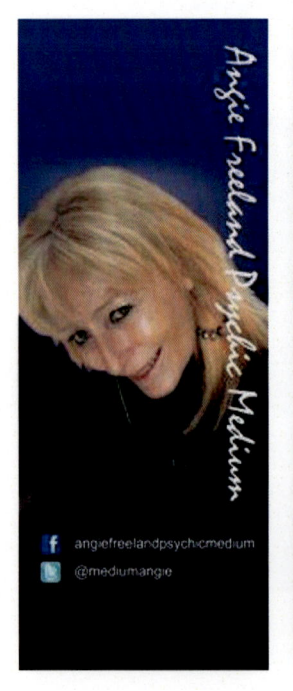

Launch publicity photographs for Angie Freeland Psychic Medium and Paranormal Troubleshooters International by Paul Page Photography

Keith and I with our little dog Snowy who, as *Between Heaven and Hell* goes to print, is 18 years old, almost blind and deaf and very unsteady on her feet but still going strong bless her.
Picture by Paul Page Photography.

Chapter 7

HEARING THEIR STORY

That little trip to the gaol was the start of many a happy and exciting investigation and I was so pleased when the manager of the gaol said we were welcome back any time. I can tell you I didn't need a second invitation!

I was itching to get back there again so we took him up on his word. We also decided to ask friends and family if they fancied joining us, after all, the more the merrier. So it was only a matter of about a week before we were back there, and this time it wasn't just going to be a walk around, we were going to investigate. It was a great night and I will always remember it fondly as it was the first full investigation we carried out at Wicklow Gaol. I've got to be honest I love that feeling that I get when we walk into a building with the intention of investigating it wondering who we're going to meet, and what they're going to say; and no matter how many times we return to investigate again, I never lose that excitement of wondering what's going to happen; and it's interesting watching those who really want to experience something from the other side of the veil, and how they react when something does happen. Interestingly enough over the years I've had many a person who has joined us for a investigation for the first time say to me how nervous they are as they're about to walk the corridors of a dark, cold building that is known to have 'ghostly goings on', but once we've started they feel completely different, and the more activity we get from spirit, the more they want.

The temperature wasn't bad in the gaol that night because it was the middle of August, and the anticipation was already building as Keith and I lead our groups into the areas we wanted to work in. The energy was nice and strong, and I could tell from the very start of our first vigil that we weren't going to be disappointed. As soon as we formed a circle and asked spirit to join us we could all feel the temperature changing around us which is normally a sign that spirit is with us, but remember this was August and it was a nice, warm evening, and yet we were all noticing how dramatically the temperature was changing, and how cold we had all started to feel. Now, I know the gaol can be on the cooler side at the best of times, but normally in the summer, if anything it can be pretty warm and stifling in some areas, like the ship area, which is where we were working at the time. This is an area at the top of what was at one time the chapel where the prisoners would go for church service and prayers. This area is now known as the ship area and is separated into two parts and is now mocked up to look like a ship. The reason for this is so that the tourists that visit the gaol can follow the story of those prisoners who were sent to the Americas and Tasmania. From the moment tourists walk through the 'gates of hell' they are walking back in time and are walking the path of so many who were interned and suffered in such horrific circumstances and for many were deported from there, and in many cases never to see their family again. Is it any wonder that there's so much unrest in the spirits that visit there as they must have had such horrific experiences!

Anyway, back to what I was saying. We formed a circle by holding hands and stood there quietly waiting for something to happen. The air smelt musty and we could hear faint little creeks on the wooden floor, wooden barrels and even from the wood that made the mock up of the captains office that had been built there, but to be honest it was just the wood swelling and creaking from the hot day we had just had.

'What's that noise?' asked one of the team members in a trembling whisper, and I was just about to explain and tell her it wasn't anything to worry about when we all jumped out of our skin from a loud bang coming from the corner behind us!

'Well it's not the bloody floorboards creaking from the heat,' I nervously answered. I immediately shouted out 'If that's you, spirit, firstly let me say thank you, and I ask if you would do that for me again please.'

We stood and waited for a few seconds when we heard it again, and this time it was even louder, but this time we were prepared for it. I could hear the gasps of peoples' breath as it happened for a third time. We were all so excited but I was also feeling a bit unnerved. As we continued to hold hands in the circle to strengthen the energy, which in turn gives spirit the energy they need to continue communicating with us, I was very aware of a man from spirit with me who was making it very clear that he was in charge; and the more I communicated with him the more I got the feeling that he was still trying to protect or guard over something that either was or still is up there and he wasn't too happy about our visit. Now, although he came through very strong he was really quite a gentle soul and was more than happy to do anything I asked of him, and one way or the other, by the time we decided to call an end to our vigil in that area, we had all experienced something. We all heard the taps and bangs, but some of the group also experienced being touched, or suddenly feeling very emotional for no reason, and we all felt the temperature changes, so all in all it was a great vigil.

Keith and his group had been holding their vigil in different cells, as there are many that are known to have an eerie feeling to them. Many times shadows that have being seen, but not only from the staff of the gaol, but from tourists who had got more than they bargained for when they paid for their entrance fee! I can tell you, I've been in those cells in the pitch black many times, and even though it may be dark make no mistake you can still see the shadows, and in many cases feel their energy so strongly as they get into your face. Not the most comfortable of feelings to experience. I've always felt that the energy in those cells holds so much heartbreak from those who interned there, and very often you can feel the fear of the children that suffered separation, isolation, hunger and fear. It must have been so hard for those that resided there, but I can't help but think how awful it would have been for children to suffer such terrible conditions, and judging by what was said by those in Keith's group, they were quite pleased the vigil was over. So it doesn't really matter whether you connect mediumistically or psychically with these poor children or the adults that would have been placed in those cells, you would have to be pretty hard not to feel the roller coaster of emotions that so many suffered.

But now we were all back together for the last vigil which was to be in the dungeon. The dungeons consist of four cells, and although they would have all been used in the past, now there's only one that we can actually go into. From the very first step we took into this dark, dingy, small and eerie cell, it was clear our energy was starting to wilt and we all agreed that it, like our energy, was being drained. I never liked that place and I remember wishing that the next hour was going to fly by, but I didn't share this with the group because I didn't want to influence their thoughts. No, they needed to experience all this for themselves.

We all made ourselves comfortable on the stone floor while we waited for something to happen. I shouted out and asked for any spirit present to let us know they were with us by giving a bang, tap etc. We all waited with baited breath and a feeling of apprehension, which was made worse because by this time we had shut the cell door to see what it felt like to be enclosed in such a suppressive, unfriendly room. To start with we had few little bangs and bumps which was great but what was really getting to us all were the feelings of despair, loneliness and hopelessness that were now becoming so overwhelming, and the longer we stayed there the worse it was getting. It had now got to the point that even though the bangs and taps had got louder and even knowing that there was a gentleman spirit amongst us it wasn't important. We had had enough! We just needed to get out! I personally felt so relieved to see that door open as we all walked towards freedom once again. If our feelings were anything to go by, those who were imprisoned there must have felt like they were on the road to hell. All in all though it had been a great night, and we had picked up so much information both from spirit and psychically that will stay with me forever.

A month later we were back there with another bunch of friends and family and as soon as I walked in I immediately felt apprehensive again. The energy felt different to the last time, and there was a strong feeling of being watched. Keith and I decided to do a walk around to get an idea of where the energy was strongest at that time.

I had started to feel a little nervous as we climbed the stairs and headed towards the ship area and my mind was racing ten to the dozen wondering what was going to happen. As I said, the chapel/ship is divided into two different parts. I believe the lower part was actually the chapel itself and the upper part was the roof of the chapel, but for some unknown reason there's always a lot of activity up there, well that's been my experience anyway, and that night became the first of many wonderful experiences the spirit there had to offer.

As we walked into the area I was very aware of a spirit gentleman whose energy was so strong he caught me unawares and pushed me followed by a very strong warning 'to stay away', but all that had done for me was to make me more determined not only to go up there, but also to hold a séance. As we broke up into small teams my apprehension was growing, even though deep down I knew that spirit couldn't harm me, I also knew they could scare the hell out of me and my team mates. I could feel the energy of this gentleman spirit around us, his energy was suffocating, and the team members were starting to comment on how oppressive the area felt. I had been a bit naughty that night because I hadn't told the others about the warning I had been given by spirit, mainly because I didn't want to scare them, and trust me when you're in the gaol with no lighting except a little torch it's very easy to be scared witless. I was a bit worried that I hadn't told them, but I still decided it was better if I kept that bit to myself for the moment.

As we stood in a circle and all joined hands asking spirit to come forward and communicate with us, I knew this gentleman was going to be more than happy to respond to our requests. Immediately the temperature dropped, people were being touched and having their hair pulled etc., which was all great because we were getting what we wanted, but there was one member of the group that was concerning me because she had started to feel very sick and light-headed. At this point I wasn't sure if it was her own fear working overtime and taking its toll or if it was spirit doing this to her, but I wasn't going to take the chance. She had the opportunity to leave but decided she wanted to stay. I could see I was going to have to keep a very close eye on her.

We were well into the séance and had had some great responses, bangs, shuffles, footsteps and moans, but my attention was more on the lady in the group who was adamant that she didn't want to break off and leave the group but my concern was that she really wasn't able to be part of it either. We were having a lot of response when asking spirit to move the glass that we were using. For those of you who are not familiar with what I mean, this is another way to work with spirit by using an ordinary glass. Turn it upside down on a table and either hover your finger over the glass or gently place the tip of your finger on the glass. I do mean gentle though, asking spirit to move the glass either for questions you want a yes or no to, or just to show they are with you. The theory is that by having your finger near or gently placed on the glass spirit can use your energy to move it. Mind you it doesn't always have to be a glass. When working with the public because of the risk of a glass flying off the table and breaking, we very often use a piece of wood called a planchette that has been made especially for this use. In fact many people prefer to use a planchette as it is believed that because it's made by hand, the energy of the person who made it resides in the wood and gives a greater energy when being used. It is a triangular shape and when fingers are placed gently over or on this piece of wood as with a glass, spirit can move it in the same way. Many people link this way of working with an Ouija board, but let me stress here that under no circumstances do we ever use an Ouija board on investigations, neither with the public, or when we're working privately.

Anyway back to my story. The uncomfortable feeling I had been having all night had started to get worse. I was still worried about my team mate and how she was feeling, and I was worried what this gentleman spirit was going to get up to next, I could just sense that he was about to pull a stunt, the problem was that I didn't know what!

My attention was more focussed on my team mate than on the actual séance; if anything was going to happen around here I needed to make sure I was able to deal with it as her energy was now very low. What happened next was I think one of the most amazing but scariest things that I have ever experienced. It was strange really because I had lost my concentration on both the séance and my team mate, and for those few moments I wasn't sure where I was, but then all of a sudden I was back in the group and I promptly looked up and over towards my team mate who had been poorly and there he was, standing behind her, just staring at me. He was tall, quite big built, and definitely a jailer. I can tell you those few seconds seemed to go on for ages, and what was worse I felt paralysed and just kept staring back at him in utter shock of what I was seeing. Even though it was dark we did have a couple of torches on and I could see him very clearly, he was not my imagination, he was very real and the fact that he stood behind the one person whose had been feeling ill and drained all the while we were working in that area convinced me even more that he had been causing her to feel ill. I started screaming out, 'Oh, my God, look!' but as soon as I said that he disappeared as quickly as he had appeared.

Yep, I had freaked. I just didn't expect that, not to see a full apparition like that. Everyone was looking around in panic and saying, 'What? What?' but because of the way some of them were standing, they had their backs to him, and the others were busy focussing on the glass moving in the séance, no-one else saw what I did, and now to add insult to injury this lovely gentleman spirit was laughing in my ear. He had succeeded in what he wanted to do and that was to scare me, even if it was only for a few moments. We continued for a while longer and was still getting activity, but because of the warning I had had earlier in the evening and now the apparition that had appeared it was time to have a break. I was feeling tired, drained and overwhelmed, I really needed to get out of there and catch my breath, take in what I had just seen and give the group a break as well as I could see that they were all getting panicky. Too much was happening all at once and I had definitely lost my grounding. Rule number one: always stay grounded at all times. So we went off for a well deserved break, and boy was I glad to get out of there!

The other groups were also having some fun experiencing shadows, smells, being touched and having a go at table tilting (table tilting has the same theory behind it as for the glass. Either by hovering our hands over the table, or placing your finger tips very gently on the edge of the table, it is believed that spirit can use our energy to move the table in different directions and at different speeds). Now I was always keen to watch this and in the past I had had a bash myself, but to be honest when the table moved I didn't connect it to my energy being physical but more to do with someone else's energy that blended well with spirit to create such a wonderful thing to happen. I mean, spirit moving the table! That to me at the time was the most amazing thing to watch.

Anyhow when we rejoined the rest of the group they were having a bash but nothing much was happening so I decided to join in. The next thing we knew the table was hopping around everywhere; it was great and I was loving every minute of it. It was only a small table that I had brought from my dad's house but it did the trick, and yes, I was keeping a very close eye on everybody's hands to make sure that no one was pushing it. And I'm sure they were all keeping a close eye on my hands also. Well, when you think about it when a table starts to move across the room, everyone is going to try a catch out who's pushing it, and trust can go out of the window very quickly. And of course mediums also have the added advantage of knowing spirit is around and whether or not they want to play ball, and I can tell you this spirit definitely wanted to play ball. The table was moving around quite fast, kept tilting on one side and finally the leg broke. Now how was I going to explain this to Dad? He didn't even know that I had borrowed the table for the night, and he would have had a pink fit if he had known what I was using it for! So poor old Keith had to come to the rescue once more and do a very quick repair job so that Dad didn't find out. It's funny if you think about it, I was in my forties and I was still afraid of how my dad was going to react.

Over the next few months we visited the gaol each time we were in Ireland and every investigation was very different, although some livelier than others. Now I had got the taste of it I wanted more. I wanted to communicate with spirit every way I could and as often as I could, wherever I could. I was still working with spirit daily with readings etc. but my passion for the paranormal was growing and getting stronger and I couldn't get enough of them. But you know, I realised very quickly how selfish I was being. There I was asking spirit to show themselves, connect and communicate with me, give us shadows, bangs etc., you know, the normal kind of things us investigators ask for, but I had to ask what was I doing for them? Spirit had never let me down, in fact they did all that I asked and more, and all I was really doing was taking. Oh, I showed them respect, but I wasn't really doing anything more for them; no I wasn't really hearing them. When I say that, what I mean is each and every spirit has a story to tell, especially those interned in places like Wicklow Gaol, and I wasn't giving them the opportunity to share with us what they had endured, what it was like for them, and more to the point are they at peace now? And do they need healing? I just wanted them to move a table or make a bang, etc. Like I said, I wasn't hearing their story, which now for me is the most important thing. We need to hear their story and understand what they went through, they have a right to be heard and through this we can learn so much. In my opinion we owe this much to spirit, and it's also part of our duty to open as many eyes that we can to share awareness and evidence that spirit provides us with to prove they live on. I realised very quickly that no matter how I was going to work for spirit the most important thing was to ensure that it was about them, and not about what they are capable of doing. Well maybe a little about what they are capable of doing. After all how could we pass on the experiences they give us, not to mention the evidence we need if we are trying to show that their energy is always around us?

On one of my visits back to Ireland things had changed. The gaol had closed and we were no longer able to do investigations there. There had been talks about closing it for a while because it had been struggling to make the money it needed to keep it going. I was gutted! I loved being there and working with spirit, and it used to give me something to look forward to every visit as it used to give us a bit of a break from looking after Dad. Now don't get me wrong, I loved being with Dad and I loved looking after him, but his health was failing and his moods were so low, which was so hard to see, and being able to go along to the gaol to do what I love the most for a few hours was a great outlet. I know there were other places in Ireland to investigate but at the time I didn't have a clue where to start, and I also didn't want to go too far out of our area in case Dad needed me, so it had to be pretty local. Thankfully in time all that changed but back then the gaol was pretty convenient.

Back in the UK, although all of my commitment and my development was paying off and I was becoming more confident and going from strength to strength as a medium, I was missing my paranormal investigations though they were very few and far between at this stage. I was getting withdrawal symptoms and this went on for about six months until a phone call we received changed all this.

As luck would have it we were visiting Dad as usual and one sunny afternoon his phone rang. 'Hello can I speak to Angie please,' said a female voice at the end of the phone.

It was the lovely Marie who worked at the gaol and who had looked after us so well when we used to do our investigations there, and now she is one of my dearest friends. Well, the long and short of this story is that thankfully the gaol had re-opened with a new manager called Martina who was working wonders in turning things around, and one of the things that she had managed to accomplish was to bring Ghost Hunters International over to investigate the gaol. Ghost Hunters International is a paranormal team that investigates haunted locations throughout the world. They also have a very successful TV show on Syfy TV, and of course it was no surprise that their findings confirmed that Wicklow Gaol is haunted. As you can imagine this was exciting stuff and all of a sudden people were taking an interest in what is reputedly 'the most haunted place in Ireland', including the media, which is why Marie had phoned me that afternoon.

'We have the press coming down for an interview and a look around at six o'clock this evening and we need a medium. Can you be here for that?' explained Marie. Well naturally we jumped at the chance.

It was great to be back there, although a little nerve racking also. If my memory serves me correctly there were only about four or five people there, mostly journalists I think.

Thankfully the evening went well and as we walked around the gaol I loved sharing all of the great experiences I had had there in the past. And of course encouraging spirit to do something to show us they were with us. As the evening drew to a close I thought my work there had been done and that would be the end of it, but no, this was only the start because we were lucky enough to be invited back to host paranormal investigations there on a monthly basis. What an opportunity, and of course we jumped at the chance. I felt so honoured to be asked, but more importantly have the opportunity to be working there with spirit again. Although Keith and I were used to running investigations with friends and family and solely for pleasure, this was different as we would be working with the public which meant there was a lot more involved, like health and safety issues and keeping them physically, mentally and emotionally safe at all times. Not an easy task when someone's freaking! It also meant that we had to move our butts very quickly and buy some more equipment as the date for the first paranormal night had been set for the following month. I couldn't wait!

As usual I was doing the worrying bit and taking myself down the 'what if this goes wrong, what if that goes wrong?' road, but as soon as we walked in I knew that spirit wasn't going to let us down. We started the evening with a walk around just to give an outline of the history and believe me that alone can be an uncomfortable feeling at times, as you don't have to wait for the lights to go out before stuff starts to happen. In fact there have been quite a few tourists who have visited for the day who have very often shared their 'strange experiences' to the staff, and this includes apparitions. So just imagine, if that stuff can happen when the gaol is full and it's broad daylight, what can happen when the lights go out and all you have is a little torch if something happens and you're inviting spirit to come and meet you? Hmm, not for the faint hearted!

Keith and I had done a separate walk around earlier in the day, and had agreed on the different areas we should work in. We always do this before an investigation, Keith with his dowsing roads and other bits of equipment and me with my mediumship and psychic abilities, and we always agree where the energy feels stronger and is a good place to hold a vigil. I wanted to work in the ship area; I don't know why but every time I go there I always want to work up there and before each investigation I always say 'I'm going to work in a different area this time,' but when I get there I always know that's where I need to be.

We broke up into our groups and as all the lights went out we started to head towards the area we were going to be working in. With each step we took I had such apprehension because I knew something was going to happen, I just didn't know what. The vigil started off very quiet and we were asking for signs and bangs, anything to let us know they were with us. Some of the group started to comment on how the energy was starting to change around them and we all agreed that it was starting to feel oppressive. I could sense a man around me, he was drawing nearer and this coincided with a huge temperature drop (always a good sign that spirit is around us). Now the activity had started to step up a bit because people were experiencing being touched. We were pretty thrilled with what we were getting so far, but at that point nothing mind-blowing had taken place.

When we went for a coffee break at the end of the vigil each group were sharing their experiences they had all had in their different groups, and it was great to see most of the people excited about what had been happening for them. I say most of the people because not everyone that comes along to the gaol is looking for proof that spirit exists, some are there to try and disprove that spirit exist and they will on some occasions try and challenge the rest of the group because of their beliefs. These cynics often try and sabotage investigations, and I have on the odd occasion threatened to throw vocal and disruptive cynics out because they were spoiling it for the rest, which is a real shame. If only they would allow themselves to be open enough to experience anything that can't be explained by science. They really do miss out on so much. Now, don't get me wrong, I'm all for scepticism and I always welcome those who are not believers but they're not non-believers and are open to whatever they experience on the investigation. After all not everything is down to spirit and it goes back to being grounded and balanced when on an investigation.

We tend to rotate the groups around every hour or so with new team leaders to give everyone the opportunity of working in different parts of the gaol, and hopefully experience different things. For me though I was going to be up in the ship all night and each group brings new and different energy, and of course the more we work up there the higher the energy levels are, all the necessary ingredients for activity.

Each time I headed up to the ship after a break I kept feeling sick because I knew that the energy was building up stronger and stronger. I could really feel it around me and I knew that spirit were making the most of it as well. In one of the séances we encountered a very angry spirit who had been a prisoner there and when working with a planchette to get yes or no answers it just went crazy. Before any of you cynics out there think that someone was pushing it I can assure you that we had a torch over the table so everybody's fingers could be seen. The more we asked this spirit questions the crazier the planchette went. It was clear that he didn't want this. Perhaps he had had enough of that when he was alive and we certainly didn't want to aggravate or upset him, but he was so great to work with. If my memory serves me correctly this spirit had been interned for murder but claimed his innocence. The séance was getting livelier by the minute and then all of a sudden we heard this massive growl that came from the centre of the circle. We all stopped immediately. We couldn't believe what we had just heard, and this time everyone had heard it. But what amazed me was that no one freaked or screamed, they just embraced all that was happening and were asking for more.

We were only a small number of people but we all worked so well together and spirit certainly enjoyed working with us. There was a lovely moment in the last session when a little spirit boy joined us and he had such fun doing table tilting with us and I'm sure the other spirits around that night were helping. The whole group including myself were so moved by the little lad and we got a real sense that he was getting more attention with us than he ever got when he was alive. He so enjoyed showing us what he could do, and he certainly made our night, but it was heartbreaking to think that he had to die and return as spirit in order to be noticed. This poor little mite was about 11-12 years old and had been imprisoned for stealing food and sadly died whilst there of a chest related illness. Yes, little Robert (that was the name he gave me) will remain in my heart and thoughts forever.

Over the years I've communicated with quite a few children that had passed through different diseases that swept through the gaol. Those poor little mites didn't stand a chance really because of the poor conditions they were living in and so many were so young. As lovely as it is to communicate with these lovely little children, it always breaks my heart to think of the awful suffering they endured. No child should ever have had to go through that. But it wasn't only Wicklow Gaol that was as bad as this. If you look back through history all gaols were the same with the most appalling conditions and harsh punishment that so many endured and I find it so upsetting to think that in some cases people were sentenced to this kind of life just for stealing food, as was the case with many of the children. I'm sure it was tough enough for the men and women to go through let along for those poor kids. But you know, even with all the sadness and suffering they experienced they're always happy to come back and spend the evening with us and show us just how amazing they are.

I can honestly say that all the spirit at Wicklow Gaol have never let us down.

Chapter 8

OH DAD!

But although life sounds very rosy for me at that time, it was far from it. In fact it was one of the worst times of my life and when I look back now I can't help but wonder how not only myself but my whole family got through it. Oh yes, things were going from strength to strength with my mediumship and in that area my dreams really were coming true, but on a personal level Dad's health was deteriorating badly. He had to have a pacemaker fitted, he was severely depressed, refusing to eat or drink and as a result his body was slowly shutting down on him. He was unable to walk and in a wheelchair, and to add to all this he was having terrible problems with his eye. One eye in particular was in a very bad way and he was slowly losing his sight in it. Each time we went over for a visit he had gone further and further downhill physically, emotionally and mentally and each night when I phoned him his conversation was getting less and less. His world had got very small, which was heartbreaking to see especially knowing there was nothing we could do to help him. He had lost interest in living and didn't want to interact with anyone including Keith and myself.

When I say he had stopped interacting with everyone I mean everyone except for one person. And boy oh boy did this person have an influence over him, and it is my opinion that it wasn't a positive influence, more like a negative one. For the purpose of this book this person shall be called Georgina for a number of reasons, and I would also stress that all that I write in this book is about my experiences throughout this dreadful situation and my beliefs around what happened based on what was happening at the time. I also want to say Dad had some great carers who looked after him well and my family were absolutely the best in helping wherever they could, and this goes for his neighbours also. So thank you all.

Georgina had been a friend of Mum and Dad's for a few years and after Mum's death Dad used to enjoy her visits, especially when she brought the children with her. Dad used to tell me how much she loved his land and apparently she had told him that if he ever wanted to sell it or if I wanted to sell it after Dad had passed over all I had to do was phone her and she would have the money ready the next day. Apparently she wanted the land for 'grazing horses' and Dad also said he was pleased that if I wanted to ever sell the property once he had passed over I had a buyer just waiting in the wings. Dad also told me of another conversation between Georgina and himself, where apparently she offered to buy his land there and then and he could either build a small house at the bottom of the field or put a caravan there for him and she would be his landlord, and if he did this, according to dad she promised that he could stay there as long as he liked. I couldn't help but think what strange conversations they were having, and I was feeling somewhat uncomfortable about the recent proposition she had put to him. Thankfully Dad did ask our opinion and I told him that I didn't think it was a good idea, and that I was feeling really uncomfortable about it all. Again, I do have to stress here that I only ever spoke to Dad about this, never to Georgina so I can only go on what Dad told me, but why would Dad lie to me? He had no reason to.

Each visit was getting tougher, and as a result of Dad not eating or drinking he was visibly growing weaker by the day. When friends and family visited him he would pretend to be asleep and he wasn't much better with us. At this point we were still visiting regularly but we also had an incredible amount of stress back in the UK as we were in the middle of selling our house for a number of reasons, the first being that Dad had given us an acre of land and he wanted us to build a property on it, for which the planning permission was just in the process of being granted. We knew that at some stage we would want to spend more time with him because of his failing health. It had taken him a year to persuade Keith and myself to accept this lovely gift and he was so chuffed when we finally agreed, but to be honest we didn't see the point of building something at the back of the house when we could stay with him. However in the end we gave in and agreed. Looking back now I see it was Dad's way of making sure we had a purpose to keep coming over to visit. I also think he believed that if we had a home over there, then we would move over there. Poor Dad, he must have felt pretty insecure and lonely. Naturally this was going to take a lot of money which would need to come from the sale of the house. But Dad wasn't the only reason we wanted to sell our house, we also wanted to finally live out our dream of spending more time in our winter home in Tenerife and also make our apartment that we had owned in Dorset for a number of years our UK home. Both Keith and I had not only dreamed about this but had worked to put this into place for as far back as I can remember and finally we were so close.

Now none of this was going to affect Dad because no matter where we were in the world we would still be doing our regular visits and phoning him every night for our normal chat, and we went to great lengths to reassure dad of this. Although Keith and I were grateful for the gift that Dad had given us, we did feel as we were letting go of one lot of pressure we were taking on a load more, but we had convinced ourselves this was all for the best especially as Dad was letting the house go to rack and ruin – it was becoming people unfriendly and he wouldn't let us do anything to change it.

Each day was becoming more stressful. What with the move and because Dad's health was declining, it was getting to the point I dreaded the phone ringing in case there was a voice on the other end telling me Dad was in hospital as this was now becoming a regular occurrence. Like the time Dad was rushed into hospital with severe dehydration and we were told the next 24 hours were going to be crucial. I was so worried; all I wanted was to be with him, so Keith and I agreed that he would stay in the UK and deal with all that was going on and I would fly over to be with him.

Thankfully he did turn the corner but when I went to see him in hospital he barely acknowledged me. I just put it down to him being exhausted and ill at the time, but at least he knew I was there, that was the main thing.

As I sat beside Dad's bed I looked over to his locker and to my surprise there was a picture of Georgina and her children on it. The nurse saw me looking at the picture and commented on what a lovely picture of his grandchildren it was. I couldn't believe my ears! Why would the nurse think they were Dad's family? And why would Georgina put a picture of herself and her kids on there? I was confused and yes, I was angry. I can tell you I was very quick in putting the nurse straight. So on my next visit I placed a picture of Mum on his locker, which did its job of hiding her photo. My gut hunch didn't feel good about this situation, but I had nothing to go on except hunches, so for the moment I had decided to keep my mouth shut.

Dad seemed to be picking up a bit and was getting quite chatty. He even asked me to cook him a meal and bring it into him along with a can of Guinness. I was so chuffed and now that he was on the up I was able to give him the good news and tell him that we had sold our house in the UK and the new owners wanted it to go through a.s.a.p. which meant we would be able to look at building our little home at the back of him. It was the first time I had seen a smile on his face in ages, and he was full of advice on the best time to start building etc. At least now he'd got something to look forward to.

I visited Dad every day and each day would be different with his moods. Sometimes he would chat away and other times he would say nothing and just lay there. On the day before I was due to go back to the UK Dad asked me to bring his cheque book in for him as he wanted to write a cheque out for our two nieces as they were both in the process of moving as well and he wanted to give them a little help. He told me he was going to give them both 10,000 Euros each. Not that he had to explain what he was spending his money on to me, it was his money and none of my business. I do remember thinking though how lovely that was, and how much it would help both the girls.

When I left that day I felt very comfortable that Dad was picking up and although we didn't know quite when he was coming home, when he did he had a good network of support that we had set up with friends, family and neighbours and of course not forgetting his carers, and it would only be another two weeks and we'd be back with him again. So I returned back to England with a mission to get on with the move.

What happened next was to change my relationship with my father forever. I was only home three days when I got a phone call from the hospital stating that my father had psychiatric problems and they wanted my permission to have him sectioned into a psychiatric unit for assessment. I couldn't believe it; the week before they were badgering me to have him placed into a home on a long term basis and now they were asking me to give permission to have him sectioned! As I had done the previous week I refused immediately. I knew that Dad would be so distraught if this were to happen and I wasn't going to play any part in it. The doctor then went on to tell me that if I didn't give my permission they would take the necessary action to have him sectioned without my permission. I made it quite clear that I didn't agree with what they wanted to do and they needed to tell my dad that I opposed it. They agreed they would tell him.

I went into immediate panic. Dad was going to be so distraught and there was nothing I could do to stop it. I phoned Georgina to tell her what was happening because I knew Dad would want her told and the reaction I got from her stunned me. She was of the opinion that I didn't do enough to prevent it, and that she didn't believe there was such a thing as a section order act. She also told me she was going straight to the hospital to prevent him going. Goodness knows what she thought she could do, after all, if his own daughter couldn't prevent it, then how the hell was she going to? By this time I was getting very angry with this woman, and I found it very strange that a friend of the family should behave in such a way. I asked her not to upset Dad because it would only make things worse for him. My gut instinct was sending out strong warning signals about this bloody woman. I didn't trust her and I knew deep down this situation was going to get worse, but little did I realise how bad it was going to get.

Although Dad didn't want to go, he settled in quite well and was interacting with the nurses. He was even reminiscing with a nurse that came from Essex where he worked and lived when he was a young man. The hospital had also reassured me that Dad was aware that I opposed this move. Dad's biggest fear was being placed into a home and he certainly wouldn't be happy with being sectioned in a psychiatric unit. I felt that he had been through enough in such a short space of time, and I didn't believe it would do him any good being sectioned. I didn't hear anything further from Georgina, and obviously she wasn't able to stop it happening. For the next couple of days I was phoning the hospital to check out how he was doing and getting reassurances that he was doing OK. But then I got a phone call to say that dad was being transferred back to Wexford Hospital because he had had a massive drop in blood pressure and was very poorly. Once again the next 24 hours was going to be critical. To my surprise when I phoned the hospital they informed me that Georgina's 17 year old daughter was keeping a daily vigil by his bedside. What the hell was going on? Georgina and her daughter were around him like bees around a honey pot, and I was like a cat on a hot tin roof!

Thankfully Dad's health became stable again, but they were going to keep him in indefinitely. Each day I would phone up the hospital to ask how he was doing and each day

Georgina or her daughter had been with him keeping a vigil. Something definitely wasn't feeling right about all of this. Why would a 17 year old girl want to keep a vigil over an old man that she had only known for a few years? None of this made sense.

It was soon time to travel back to Ireland and I couldn't wait to get there to see Dad. The night before we travelled I phoned the hospital as I always did and they told me he was quite bright today, and asked me if I would like to speak to him. Naturally I jumped at the chance, but when the nurse told him who it was and tried to hand the phone to him I could hear Dad saying, 'No, I don't want to speak to her, I never want to speak to her again.'

While I was waiting at the other end of the phone I was panicking as I overheard all that he had to say. Eventually the nurse managed to get him to take the phone and speak to me. 'Dad what's wrong?' I asked. 'What have I done wrong?'

Nothing could have prepared me for what he said next.

'You've done the dirty on me; there's too many secrets and I never want to speak to you again.'

My world had just fallen apart. I knew Dad well enough to know when he made his mind up there would be no changing it, and I've also seen him turn on people in the past for reasons only known to him, and has never spoken to them again.

Keith wasn't at home when all this happened and when he returned he walked in to find me sobbing my heart out to the point I could barely breathe. I had no idea what I was supposed to have done. Keith immediately phoned the hospital to see if the nurse could enlighten us, but she also had no idea why he turned like that, and I think she was quite embarrassed to be witness to it all. Keith was hoping that all this could be sorted out once we got to Ireland the next day, but I knew that wasn't going to happen. Dad had made his decision and he never went back on one.

Once I got myself together Keith persuaded me to phone Georgina to see if she could shed any light on all of this, but all she could say was, 'You were his next of kin, you should have done more.' She also went on to say, 'We got him out of there, it was Deirdre's soup (Deirdre is her daughter) that brought him around.' She went on to say that my father believed I had 'put him in the looney bin'. What the hell was she going on about? Here she was taking the credit for getting him transferred to Wexford hospital because of her daughter's soup, and it's miracle cure. I've heard it all now! When I challenged this she then changed her story and said Dad was transferred 'due to his medical condition'. It also transpired that Georgina was with him when he first took bad in the psychiatric unit, but hadn't contacted me to let me know what was happening. That night felt like one of the longest in my life. Over and over again I was going through the situation. How could he think I would do that to him?

As we travelled across to Ireland the next day I had a gut feeling we were heading into a minefield. I knew there was more to this situation than met the eye. Although Dad wasn't speaking to me we still stayed at his house as he was still in hospital. The next day Keith and I decided that he would go to see dad on his own to talk to him to try and find out what was going on and to talk him round, but deep down I knew he would have more chance of flying to the moon.

Keith could see how weak Dad was and as Dad saw Keith standing there, his first words to him were, 'You've been good to me. I want you to have the land but it will have to go through Angela's name.'

When Keith asked him why he didn't want anything to do with me his reply was, 'She put me in the 'looney bin and she stopped the four cheques I wrote out for Georgina's four children because she thinks I'm of unsound mind.'

What the hell was he going on about? I didn't even know he wrote out four cheques for the total sum of 20,000 Euros for her children, let alone stop them, but how was I going to persuade Dad of this? Keith promised Dad he would have a word with the bank to find out what had happened.

When we visited the bank they explained that they have a duty of care to elderly clients to protect them so if they see a large amount of money coming out of an elderly person's account they put a stop on all cheques etc. until they have investigated the situation and are happy that nothing untoward is happening. So it was the bank that stopped the cheques because of the amount of money the cheques were written out for. They were also happy to write a letter for us to take up to him explaining everything.

The day we took the letter up to show Dad it was his birthday. We also had a meeting with his doctor, as he wanted to discuss Dad's welfare and where we went from there. The doctor had also invited Georgina and her husband to attend as he felt she could be valuable as part of the care system as she was the only one who could get him to eat or drink. It took me all my strength to be in the same room as her let alone speak to her. Georgina and her husband were vocal in their opinion of me as a daughter and at one point Georgina's husband called us 'casual visitors'. According to them, we should have just dropped everything and moved over. They also felt that our regular visits weren't enough. WTF! Who the hell were they to tell us what we should and shouldn't do, and how we should do it? I was fuming! All I wanted to do was rip their heads off, and believe me, at that time it would have been the easiest thing to do, but Dad's health was more important. Plus, I wasn't going to give her the pleasure of running to Dad and twisting the knife in even further by telling him that I had lost the plot! So I kept my cool, only just though.

Dad had been diagnosed with passive death wish, and paranoia; apparently 'the worst case they had ever seen.' Passive death wish is a form of depression where the person loses the will to live and obsesses about dying, but has no intention of killing themselves, but they stop eating and drinking, which causes the body to close down over a period of time.

It was bloody awful to watch a man who had been so strong physically and mentally, and who had always shown great will power slowly dying because he had had enough of life. By this time Dad's paranoia was getting worse, and although he always had an issue with money and its importance, he had become totally obsessed with it, and I frequently got told by those that would visit him in hospital he would very often lie in his bed and count the money in his purse, just in case someone had taken it. He became obsessed with the thought that we were all after his money and land. The poor man. It was tearing me apart that he was going through all this, and yet according to them I was a useless and uncaring daughter.

The agreement made that day was that Keith and I would look at having 24/7 care put into place for him and Georgina was going to talk Dad around to re-establishing my relationship with him, but I wasn't going to hold my breath, especially if she was in charge of getting Dad to realise my innocence, but for now I just had to carry on regardless for Dad's sake. Before the meeting Keith popped into see Dad with the letter from the bank, but as I feared Dad wasn't interested. Regardless of what the letter said he still believed I had him sectioned and that I also stopped the cheques. There appeared to be nothing I could do or say that would persuade him I was innocent.

After the meeting had finished I desperately wanted to go in and see Dad but I knew by the welcome that Keith got earlier that I definitely wouldn't be welcome. He would either have sworn at me or just ignored me, and I wasn't strong enough for that either. I was falling apart. All of this was breaking my heart, and to add to this heartbreak, after the meeting had finished Georgina appeared to be having great delight in telling me her daughter had made a cake for him, and she was rushing around trying to find a vase for the flowers that she had bought him. There were no words to describe how I felt at that point. I couldn't believe all of this was happening and to watch someone else play the daughter, doing all the things I should be doing was one of the worst experiences of my life. But again I had to try and focus on what we had to do for Dad.

So Keith and I promptly started searching for a company that provided a good 24/7 care support system and we were so lucky because we found a company that ticked all the boxes, and they could start immediately, although we knew it wasn't going to be cheap. As promised I phoned Georgina to keep her in the loop but surprise, surprise, she didn't seem to approve, mainly because of 'cost' but also because she knew someone who was a nurse/carer that could look after Dad. It seemed any decision I made wasn't approved of by Georgina.

Keith and I were due to return to England but before we did we decided to have another meeting with Dad's specialist to give him an update. It was at that meeting that the doctor told me he would be surprised if Dad was still here in six months. His body had endured so much over the last few months and was closing down. To receive this news under natural circumstances was hard enough but to be told this under these circumstances was unbearable. We had a feeling Dad was slowly dying but to have it confirmed was something else. Now the need to resolve this situation was even more important and to do that I had to rely on a woman I neither liked nor trusted.

Keith and I didn't have to do any thinking, we knew that we wanted to move over to be with him and told the doctor this. He was really pleased and as we started to talk about the way forward and how to get the best support for Dad, we realised that our daughter Katie would be invaluable as she had been trained to work with elderly people and had worked in care homes previously. Obviously though we would have to get her agreement. At the time she was living in Tenerife, but was terribly unhappy because she had lost her job in a bar/restaurant due to the tourist trade and the economy being hit so hard over there, which meant they could no longer keep her on; and there was very little prospect of her trying to find another position. But the main reason for her sadness was because she was missing the family so much. Katie is very much a family and home girl, and although she was OK for a short while, she hated being away from everyone, so naturally she jumped at the chance to be looking after her granddad. So it was all agreed we would book a one way sailing ticket for Ireland for three weeks time. It was a scary time, but there was a huge part of me that was relieved we had made this decision because I so wanted to be with Dad to look after him, but there was another part of me that was very apprehensive.

The move was going smoothly and we were busting a gut trying to get things done as quickly as possible, plus it was keeping my mind busy as I needed to keep my mind off things otherwise I was going to go under. I had already started to lose a lot of weight; I wasn't eating, and anyone that knows me knows how I love my food, and I certainly wasn't sleeping.

Georgina wasn't helping matters as it didn't appear that she was keeping her side of the agreement. There were many times when she would ignore any texts I sent her asking if she was talking to Dad about my innocence. And also about bringing him around to the idea of us coming over to look after him. And other times she would just send a text saying either Dad wasn't in good form or the timing wasn't right. In fact there was one time when I phoned the hospital and they told me that he was a lot brighter and sitting up in a chair talking away to Georgina. I text her straight away asking her to speak to Dad, but I didn't receive a text back until the next day telling me Dad wasn't in good form so she didn't 'push the issue'. I was getting more and more frustrated with this bloody woman! Why the hell was she holding back? What could she be getting from keeping a father and his daughter separated? By the time all this was going on we knew the doctor had told Dad we were moving over to look after him, and he also reassured Dad that he would still have all his carers that he was fond of, and Georgina would also be part of the care system. But something else seemed to be going on because we found out that at some point Dad had been visited by the carer that Georgina had mentioned earlier. Why weren't we being told about this? So many questions and not enough answers.

Both Keith and I knew deep down that something was going on and we spent a lot of time trying to fathom it out. Each day would bring a new twist and turn and it always seemed that Georgina was behind it, and yet another day of twists and turns was just about to happen.

Our niece Michelle text us; she was so confused and upset because once again she didn't know what to do with what had just happened. Apparently she had just had a text from one of Dad's carers stating that Dad wanted her to visit him in Ireland and he wanted her to do it before we arrived. Dad also called her just moments after she received the text and told her she wasn't to speak to Keith or myself about this, that Georgina would take her straight to his solicitor where she would need to sign some papers, and then Georgina would bring her out to the hospital to visit him. Michelle asked what it was all about but he seemed very unclear. Our gut feeling that something underhand was going on had just got even stronger, and I was feeling sick to the pit of my stomach. This was one hell of a puzzle and none of the pieces were fitting.

Over the next few days I was texting Georgina asking if she was any further forward, but we still kept getting the same old crap, either she wouldn't respond or she would just say we needed to give Dad time to get used to the situation. We also felt our hands were tied because we had promised Michelle that we wouldn't let on that we knew about the texts and phone calls that she was getting from Dad, his carers, and Georgina, just in case he decided to disown her as well. I knew he was capable of that, and I didn't want her to experience what I was feeling. So we had to keep quiet. I didn't know how much more of this I could take. We were on the verge of moving our home down to Dorset and then just four days later we would be boarding a ferry and moving over to Ireland and all the indications at this point were that we were definitely not welcome.

I felt so desperate, and so let down by Dad, and by Mum for leaving us and not helping with this situation with Dad. I was hurting badly and although I had a huge amount of support from everyone I still felt so alone. In my quieter moments I would call on Mum and Lou to come forward, in fact I would actually beg them to come forward and let me feel their presence, just to let me know they were with me, but nothing. On the surface I was so angry but more than anything I was so scared because I didn't know how or when all this crap was going to end. I got so bad that I would dread going to bed because I couldn't sleep and I would dread getting up because I had to face another day. I was exhausted and I felt as though I had lost all the fight I had in me.

There was one night in particular when once again I couldn't sleep and things seemed darker than ever before. I was sore from crying and I felt like I had been brought to my knees. I just didn't know how to get up or even if I could. At that moment just for a brief while I remember thinking what's the point? For that short moment in time I didn't want to carry on. Yep, I had been broken and I didn't want to live to face it anymore – no more getting up to face the crap that's being flung at us, no more sleepless nights and no more pain, no more rejection from a man I knew as my father. I'll never forget that moment of desperation, that brief moment of madness of wanting to go to sleep and never wake up. But it was also at that moment when something inside me snapped and I realised that nothing, but nothing is worth that. I knew I was innocent and I was going to stand up and fight no matter what it took, and I realised that even though this was one of my darkest times, every breath from now on was going to give me the strength I needed to carry on and be counted no matter what!

You know that saying: 'You may be down, but you're not out'? Well, that was the new determination I had found when I realised how close I was to rock bottom. I had made my mind up in that split second that nothing, but nothing was going to get the better of me! I knew I wasn't going to be able to carry on as normal with everything that was happening, so I decided I needed to find a new 'normal' for me.

At first it was bloody hard to carry on like nothing was happening, and on many occasions took all my strength to not give in, but I was determined never to let this situation get the better of me. I wasn't going to allow my life to be destroyed. I had too much to live for.

At this time my connection with spirit was more important to me than ever, and I did my best to make damn sure that none of this crap got in the way. Throughout all this I regularly sat with spirit; just to feel their presence made such a difference to how I was feeling. My guides would visit me regularly with words of wisdom and encouragement, which gave me such strength and motivation to keep on going; but to be honest it was my mum or sister that I desperately wanted to feel around me, just to know they were there. That sounds so ungrateful on my guides, but I know they understood. As I look back now, I realise that, what I actually wanted was for them to come back and make everything OK again, but of course that wasn't going to happen. I was missing them badly, and it hurt so much that they were physically no longer with us, and to be honest I was angry with both of them for not connecting with me or letting me know they were near. I used to pray every night for them to come close, but for a while it felt like those prayers weren't being heard. Until, finally, one evening while I was sitting quietly on my own, Mum came to visit; and oh boy, what a visit it turned out to be!

I had been hoping for a loving, comforting message that would keep me going, but all I got instead was Mum pointing her finger at me in an angry way (a typical trait of Mum's if she was annoyed!). It felt like she was really angry at me for not dealing with this situation the way she would have, which to be honest, would have been to have a big blow up with Georgina, and the chances were high she probably would have ended trying to punch her lights out! I wasn't having any of this finger wagging lark, or the bad mood she was showing, and in no uncertain terms, I told her to back off and leave me alone. I have to say I said a few other things as well. At first I went around muttering away to myself saying, 'How bloody dare she? etc., etc. And I must admit I felt awful afterwards, but at the time I was so vulnerable that to feel even Mum could attack me from spirit was a bit too much to take. I had had enough of constantly defending myself to everyone.

That awful feeling of hurt about what had happened lasted for a few days, and I kept asking myself why. Why would she be so hard on me? I couldn't work it out, and it was only after I had a beautiful connection with my guide when he pointed out to me that I had totally misread that message from Mum that day; bless her, all she wanted to do was give me the support and guidance I was looking for, but because I was so bloody angry with myself for letting all this stuff happen, and deep down I was blaming myself, that I didn't stop to take in all that she was telling me. I just assumed by the finger wagging that she had the hump! A lesson learned; stop and listen to what I'm being told, not only from those who have passed, but also from those who are living. I had put my own interpretation on that message because of how I was feeling about myself, and as for showing herself wagging her finger, well, that was because she knew normally that would have been the only time I would take in what she was saying to me because I knew she meant it. I felt so bad that I treated Mum that way that I spend the rest of the week going around apologising to her for the way I treated her. 'Sorry, Mum, I didn't mean it' and 'Sorry, Mum, I should have listened more,' was all that you would have heard me saying to myself, because I knew she would hear me. I tell you, if anybody had seen me that week they would have thought I was off my trolley! Thankfully, Mum has visited me a few times since that evening, not only through me, but through other medium's as well, and has since given some lovely messages.

The investigations at the gaol were going from strength to strength. Each investigation was becoming more active than the last one, which soon became known to those who were interested in the paranormal world, and more and more people wanted to join us to experience it for themselves. When I look back now, we had some great nights and some great memories and so many things happened that still to this day amazes me. Like the time when I was communicating with a man of the cloth who had rather an angry streak to him, and wasn't as innocent as his collar would make you believe; and of course me being me, pointed this out to him, which was a big mistake. I think everyone there had a personal experience that night, from being touched, to having someone either blow or grunt in their ear.

The energy was charged so we decided to see if our preacher friend would use our energy to do some table tilting. Oh boy, did he! It actually got to the point where the people who were around the table were struggling to keep their fingertips on the table. He was going ballistic! His party trick was to keep ramming into people and actually hurting them. He would go on one leg and swing around like mad. You could tell every movement was an angry movement, and you could feel the anger in the air, and for the first time ever I was angry and antagonistic towards him, which is so against how I believe spirit should be treated. Well, I had obviously annoyed him because the next thing I heard was 'I'm, going to hurt you,' and I knew it came from him, and to be honest I don't blame him for feeling that way.

I told the group what he had said and I shouted back all cocky 'You know you can't do that spirit, no matter how hard you try!' But this spirit was going to prove a point, even if it wasn't immediate. It was the end of the night and we were all exhausted and a bit dismayed by the end of the session, and I for one was very glad it was over. Keith had been present for most of that session so he had seen how I had behaved. Once we were on our own he told me how surprised he was at the way I treated spirit that night, and how out of character it was for me. I must admit I didn't realise until he pointed it out to me, and he was right, it was out of character and I was out of order to treat spirit that way, and I would have been very quick in condemning others for it. To this day I don't know what had come over me, but I was really sorry, and spent another day going around feeling bad and saying 'Sorry,' in the hope that spirit would forgive me.

A few days later I was back in the gaol, only this time it was to give one to one readings in a room that the manager of the gaol very kindly allowed me to use for readings and workshops.

As soon as I walked in I could feel this gentleman of the cloth around me again, and I remember wondering if he was back for round two, even if I had said sorry a thousand times. The morning went well, and as always spirit gave some fabulous evidence to their loved ones, along with beautiful messages that I could see were bringing great comfort. Before I knew where I was lunch break had been and gone. Before starting again I quickly nipped to the loo as you do and it was only when I was washing my hands and I looked up into the mirror that I noticed my left eye seemed to be quite black. I thought at first I had smudged my mascara, but no matter how hard I tried I couldn't wash the black that was under my eye away, until in the end I had to leave it because my next client was due. I settled back into my readings for the afternoon and thought no more about it, but at the end of the day when Keith came to pick me up he greeted me with 'What the hell have you done to your eye? Have you seen it?'

I looked at him like he had two heads, and asked, 'What the hell are you talking about? There's nothing wrong with my eye;' but he urged me to go and take a look. I couldn't believe it when I took a look in the mirror. I had a black eye, a real shiner! I knew I hadn't hurt it, and it wasn't sore, but I still racked my brains trying to remember if I had banged it or anything, but I knew I hadn't; and then I heard those words again, 'I'm going to hurt you', and it was at that point I knew it was my preacher friend. I had felt him around all day, and now he had got his own back!

I walked around for 10 days with a lovely shiner, and I can tell you, putting up with all those corny old jokes about my husband doing it to me became so old and boring. I still have to stick to what I say though. He didn't hurt me, and he couldn't hurt me, but he could and he did mark me. He got his point across, and I couldn't help but chuckle to myself how he had proved his point, and good on him for doing so, because I deserved it!

Chapter 9

HOW THE WORM TURNS!

Our niece Michelle had decided that she couldn't travel to Ireland at such notice because of the commitments she had at home, so she phoned Georgina to tell her. She also asked her why there was such a need for her to be in Ireland at such short notice anyway. According to Georgina Dad had plans for her over the next six months or so, but wasn't any clearer than that.

I wanted to find out more without dropping Michelle in it, so I phoned Georgina myself but this time I was going to tape the call just in case. Georgina was very quick to tell me Dad knew we were coming over but he was looking at other options other than us looking after him. She wasn't divulging anything about Michelle or Dad wanting her over there in such a hurry but I did ask her whether or not the cheques had been cashed yet. Her answer was no, she hadn't done anything about it, and yet I know for a fact that the cheques had been cashed 15 days earlier and because the cheques were in the names of her children she had to sign them for them to be banked into her account. So now I had it on tape that she had lied.

Time was getting close to us leaving for Ireland and we were still no further ahead. I had an awful feeling we were going to turn up at Dad's ready to move in and he was going tell us to f*** off, and trust me, I know Dad well enough to know he was more than capable of doing such a thing.

OK, enough is enough! I decided to call the hospital myself and insist on talking to Dad. At first when I called Dad was asleep, but I stressed how important it was so they agreed to get him to call me back when he woke. I was a nervous wreck waiting for the phone to ring. I wasn't sure if I was doing the right thing but something needed to break. For my own peace of mind I had to find out what the hell was going on. As the phone rang my heart was beating so fast, my hands were shaking, and God knows what my voice sounded like. As I said hello the nurse replied, 'Hello Angela, I have your father for you. I had to dial the number for him.'

The next minute I heard his voice, my heart melted. He still seemed confused even though he knew the nurse made the call for him. Once he realised it was me he asked me... no he *told* me to phone Michelle and tell her when she arrives on the Friday (he obviously wasn't aware yet that she wasn't coming) Georgina would take her up to the house and collect his car, then she had to go for his dog who was being looked after by his carer and then go to the hospital to collect him. I didn't want to get him off side so I agreed to do all that he said, and then I took the bull by the horns and asked 'What about Keith, Katie and myself? We're moving over to look after you.'

His reply to that was 'As long as you keep your f****** mouth shut, there will be no arguments,' and he rang off before I could get a chance to ask him anything.

Obviously his feelings towards me hadn't changed, and either he didn't care that I knew or he was just so desperate to make sure Michelle got his instructions and was expecting me to just go along with it. One thing was for sure though, Dad was obviously planning to get home five days ahead of our arrival, and if I'm to believe all that I was being told by our niece, which I did, Georgina was colluding with him to make sure this happened. The pieces of the jigsaw were starting to fit at last and I now also understood why a carer/friend of Georgina visited Dad whilst he was in hospital. It was my belief that it wasn't just a casual visit from her so see how he was, but to organise when she would be needed to look after him and this belief was strengthened when Keith phoned the hospital to speak to Dad's doctor.

When Keith first explained the doctor couldn't understand why we were so upset, and he agreed that yes, Dad was going home five days early, and he was going to be looked after by his granddaughter until we arrived. It was only when Keith explained that the granddaughter he had arranged to pick him up and take him home wasn't our daughter, who was part of the care plan we were putting into place, but his other granddaughter Michelle, who knew nothing about these arrangements.

Now because Dad was fragile physically, emotionally and mentally and he needed a lot of looking after, the doctor had the right to refuse to let him go home if he wasn't happy with any arrangements that were being made for Dad's welfare. And because he was led to believe that it was our daughter Katie who was coming over ahead of us to take Dad home and settle him in before we got there he was more than happy to let Dad go home. I don't think he was very happy to say the least. He reassured us that he wouldn't be letting Dad go home until we had arrived.

Keith then had to break the news that we had had enough of all the dirty work that we believed was going on behind our backs. It was making me ill, and let's face it, it was never going to work with all the animosity that was going on. I really felt for Michelle when all this came to light. It appeared she wasn't going to have a say in what happened next and was just expected to go along with it, and it would have been so heartbreaking for her if she let her granddad down. So it appeared with all that we were being told, while we were home busting a gut to get things done so we could move over to Ireland, there was an incredible amount of plotting going on without a care to what it would do to Michelle, her partner and children, and also Keith, Katie and myself for that matter.

This was all the last straw for me. Now was my turn to get on the phone to Georgina and have a go. I still had to be careful for Michelle's sake but I could still let her know in no uncertain terms what I thought of her and the part we believed she played in this little 'game'.

Once she realised I knew, she started to stutter, 'I-I thought you knew,' knowing full well I didn't. I wanted to say so much more than I actually did, but I knew the chances were high that I would slip up and get Michelle in the dog house. I also didn't give her the chance to say too much back. No, this was my time and she was going to have a taste of how I felt. Did it feel good? A little I guess, but not hugely because it hadn't sorted out the situation for me. All I had done was lose my cool, but I am proud that I didn't go too far and get abusive and trust me at that point it would have been so easy to do that! I was so upset that we weren't going over to look after Dad, but deep down I knew it was for the best.

Oh yes, we were still going to Ireland a few days later as planned because we had work commitments and we weren't about to let anyone down but we weren't going to be seeing Dad and we were going to be returning to England afterwards. I had given up hoping that Dad was going to see the light. There was nothing I could do so as hard as it was we just had to carry on.

So two days later we moved down to Dorset and for the first time in a while we had a bit of secure direction. Don't get me wrong, I wasn't going to cut myself off completely, I was still in touch with Dad's carers who were keeping me up updated on him and of course I was phoning the hospital every day to find out how he was. I knew all of this was going to hurt but nothing would hurt as much or was more frustrating as when I used to phone the hospital at a time when Georgina was with him and the nurses used to say, 'His daughter is with him right now.' Grrrrrr!

We stayed at my cousins' when we returned to Ireland, which felt really strange. This was the first time I had ever been over there and not stayed at Mum and Dad's. We had been asked a few times by members of the family if we would like to stay with them, but I never felt I could in case Dad needed me. As soon as we got there it was hectic with work and thankfully was going so well in that department. We had our regular investigations at the gaol which were packed out with a waiting list of people wanting to join us. I was also booked solid with one-to-one readings and a growing waiting list for those as well.

The manager of the gaol said half jokingly, 'We need you over here for a while.' Keith and I glimpsed at each other straight away and I could see we were thinking the same thing. If we were to come over and rent a place locally we could clear the back log of work and but be near just in case. I realised at that point that although Dad had let go of me I wasn't prepared to let go of him, and although I couldn't be part of his life right now because of all that had happened I could at least be nearby and it would be easier to keep in touch with his carers.

So it was all change again and we set about finding a little place to live in Wicklow for a few months. Luck was on our side because we found a place just 50 yards up from the gaol, thanks to my lovely cousins as they chose it for us. Perfect! Although we didn't move over straight away we were spending more time in Ireland. I still hadn't got used to being so close to Dad and not seeing him, but thankfully Dad's carers were making it a little bit easier by keeping in touch with me.

Although I wasn't smiling very often I made sure I wasn't all doom and gloom either and being able to carry on working was such a huge help to me. For that brief while I could forget all the crap in my life and enjoy the privilege of working with spirit and the comfort spirit gave to their loved ones with their wonderful messages. Life had to go on and I was going to do the best I could, so when I went to work I left all of that stuff behind me, which wasn't easy for the first while, but in time it got easier, and each message I had the privilege of passing on from spirit to their loved ones, re-instilled and strengthened my faith and beliefs in how much support and guidance spirit gives us in our toughest times.

Dad did get home and a care system was put into place by Georgina who had apparently promised to set it up and make sure it would run smoothly. Michelle was doing a great job at getting over as much as she could but Dad was getting more and more frail with every day that passed. It had recently transpired that Dad had decided to transfer the deeds of the house and land over to Vikki which was the reason why he was keen to get her over to Ireland and sign some papers. I guess the way he was thinking at that time was if it was all in her name before he passed then it couldn't be contested when he passed, although I can't say that for sure, again it's just my perception of what was happening at the time. There was one point when he asked Michelle if she wanted the house and land or 'would it be a rope around her neck?' If so he would 'give it all to someone else'. Hmm I wonder who that may have been. Keith, myself and my family discussed this situation and we all believed that the best thing that could happen at that time was for our niece to agree to all that Dad wanted to make sure it stayed in the family and when the sad day came that Dad was no longer with us the house would be divided out between my brother Frank, Michelle, her sister Sue and myself. It was an awful thing to discuss at that time but we all really believed that if Dad hadn't have been so ill psychologically it would have been what he would have wanted, and I know for sure it definitely would have been what Mum wanted.

The more time I spent over in Ireland the more I was hearing about things that didn't seem right at Dad's, and the tales I was being told about what was going on was so upsetting, I couldn't help but ask myself how the hell this was all going to end. But for a short time there was a little bit of light at the end of the tunnel when it looked like Dad was coming around. It was during one of Michelle's visits to Dad, her partner Dave was sitting with him when all of a sudden Dad looked at him and said, 'Angela should be here now. Are they coming to see me?'

Dave said, 'No, but do you want them to come over?'

Dad just said 'They know where I am.'

When Michelle told me I really thought I was in with a chance and it sounded like he was missing me and I asked her to tell him if he wanted me there I would be. Oh God, I was so excited that he may agree, but Michelle spoke to him time and time again asking him if he wanted me there, but each time she brought up my name he just closed his eyes and ignored her. Bless her heart, she felt so bad for me and once again I was breaking with the hurt and I knew it wasn't any good just turning up because he would just tell me where to go again. Just that little window of light had knocked me back so far my emotions were all over the place. I just couldn't keep going through this rejection, so I decided that although I would jump and be there, I wasn't going to ask or beg for him to see me anymore.

Life seemed so surreal at that time. One minute I would be asked to give an interview on the radio or I was in the papers because of a very active investigation we had at the gaol and the next minute I was having phone calls with either Michelle or Dad's carers about his health and what was happening. I can tell you it wasn't doing a lot of good for my nerves. But it was my quietest times that were the worst; the moments when I allowed myself to feel just how much I missed Dad. We had become so close after Mum had passed and I loved being with him. I used to joke with Keith and say, 'Dad is the only man on this earth that could say jump and I would ask how high!' I would have done anything for him. I certainly shed a few tears over all this, but I also spent a lot of time reminding myself of the blessings I had in life, especially my family, and how lucky was I to be able to work for spirit. All this kept me strong, although there were times I would get angry with everyone including spirit but on the whole my beliefs didn't falter. Please believe me, I'm not writing this in the hope that you will all feel sorry for me, but more because I want to share with you the experiences that I've had that have proved when we're up against it if we hold onto our beliefs and stay strong we will come through the other side stronger and more capable than ever before.

I wasn't only missing Dad though, I was still missing Mum and Lu-Lu as well, and as time went on I was getting more and more upset and, yes, angry with the pair of them, because I really needed to feel them near me. I can remember there was one night as I went to bed after a hell of a day I begged them to just give me a sign that they were there. Anyway, about 10 minutes later when I was already half asleep we both heard a loud bang in our bedroom, but the laugh was that we were both so exhausted that neither of us opened our eyes or got up to find out what it was. We just said, 'What's that?' to each other, and because neither of us knew, we just left it. Just imagine if that had been someone breaking in. A fine pair we would have made just sleeping through it! However, the next morning when I got up, lying on the floor on my side of the bed was a rather large fang shun crystal that we have hanging on our bedroom window. That may not seem such a big deal, but for me it does when you consider that the window isn't directly by the bed and we also have vertical blinds from ceiling to floor with no room for anything to roll under, plus the blinds were closed with no gaps and no room for it to roll through or under. And to add to that the crystal ball and the crystal thread it hangs from had been laid out so nicely. I knew this was Mum and Lu-Lu and any doubts I had been having just disappeared. I should have realised they would never let me walk alone through this minefield without being by my side and holding my hand. I realised somehow in some way they were guiding me and I just needed to trust, which as we all know, is sometimes so hard when we feel as though our life is falling apart. I did feel guilty that I doubted them, but I guess it's only natural at times especially when we feel at our weakest and most vulnerable times.

Things weren't going so well for Dad and the care system that had been set up for him was breaking down. When I spoke to one of his carers one Saturday afternoon apparently they were having trouble getting carers for him for the weekend. According to the carer four or five days earlier Georgina had gone away supposedly for a couple of days but hadn't returned, and being as she was in charge of the rota nobody knew what they were doing, there were no carers rostered for him. She had left Dad in such a vulnerable place. Thankfully we were in Ireland and if needs be we could look after him. Apparently the carer had spoken with Georgina earlier who supposedly said she was only responsible for the setting up of the care system to get him home, and now she believed the rest was up to Michelle. This was a very different story to the one we had been told by doctors and carers! With the evidence that I had, my question was why would she leave Dad so open and vulnerable? Especially when I thought about all the times she stepped in and interfered when we were trying to look after him!

Luckily, between all the carers they devised a rota to ensure that someone was with him all of the time, but that wasn't the point. I was furious but I was more worried about what would happen if she did this again. I just couldn't let this go by without saying something. I did think about phoning her, but I knew the chances were she wouldn't answer the phone so I text her instead stating that she either does what she promised or passed it onto us so that we could look after him properly. I have to say though, I didn't stop there. I also told her I blamed her fully for the breakdown between me and my dad because of her lies that I had found out about. I think I spent a considerable amount of time that afternoon texting her but for me it was worth it just to make it very clear to her that I was around, and believe me those that know me know I'm not one for tact! Surprisingly, I didn't get a response.

Based on what I had been told by the carer I couldn't help but wonder why there was such a change in her. Michelle was visiting Ireland regularly and had become the co-ordinator of the rota systems etc. to the best of her ability, keeping in mind that she lived in the UK, but she was feeling a lot of pressure from Georgina to be over there fortnightly, and apparently Georgina was texting her quite frequently asking why she wasn't over. It really does seem that the expectation was drop everything, do as you're told and move over here regardless of the commitments you have. So now our poor niece was getting it in the ear. Georgina's husband was also not a happy man because of my texts and as a result he and Keith had a very long, very heated conversation over the phone where he turned around and said, 'We could have had the lot off you if we wanted to.' What a strange thing to say! And why would a person want to say that? What was his meaning? I know I've got my perception of what that statement meant.

As I said earlier, the care system for Dad was faltering and during one of Michelle's visits Georgina seemed quite keen to change Dad's care and apparently she had the idea that a full-time carer could live in his house and that would cut the cost considerably, but papers would need to be prepared and signed giving the carer full permission to continue living there for up to 11 months after Dad had passed, and she had the very person in mind who could do this job! This seemed quite a strange set up. I'm not saying it doesn't happen but I hadn't heard of it before and I was very worried that this may be put in place, but thankfully nobody, including the carers, thought it was a good idea, except Georgina of course. Apparently Dad's carers were also quite concerned the gentleman that Georgina had in mind wasn't qualified or experienced enough. Poor old Dad, all this was going on around him and meanwhile he was getting weaker and weaker. I had heard that he was ignoring everyone including his friends that he thought the world of.

Yet again Dad was taken back into hospital and I had the honour of looking after his little dog Betty, who I loved, for a few days. This meant going up to Dad's to spend time with her and letting her out etc. It was strange being up there again. I kept thinking of all the memories we had there, especially since Mum died and how we had supported each other through it all. Oh, how I wished Dad was there for me to see him. He didn't even know it was me looking after Betty.

What was becoming apparent now was that Georgina wanted to pull back on her responsibilities of caring for Dad. On the surface it seemed that ever since the deeds of the house had been signed over to Michelle her interest was waning. Maybe Georgina thought now that Michelle was in charge she wasn't needed as much and would leave the rest to her. Who can say what was going on for her, and only she knows that, but once again I have my views about this. What gobsmacked me though was a phone call I had from her. I had just finished a day of readings and was quite excited because we were going back to the UK the next morning for a couple of weeks. Naturally I had my phone switched off and as I turned it back on there had been two or three texts from Georgina. I hadn't even had the chance to read them when the phone rang and as I saw her name flashing at me from my phone, I hesitated as to whether or not to answer it because I didn't want another row. My curiosity got the better of me and I answered it, expecting some form of back lash, but what I got was a cheery voice on the end of the phone.

'Hello Angie, it's Georgina. I've been thinking, it's about time we let bygones be bygones.'

Well you could have knocked me down with a feather. She went on to tell me that Dad was coming home that evening and she thought I should go along and pick him up! I asked her if Dad knew about this call and she said no. When I asked her what happens if Dad throws a load of verbal at me, and let's face it the chances of that happening were high, she just replied, 'Just say 'OK, Dad, and leave.'

So I was going to put myself through all of that torment just to suit her, and just think of the distress it could cause Dad. I don't think so! But I wanted to make sure I was making the right decision so I told her I would get back to her.

Keith and I had a long discussion about it but we knew the answer had to be no, for all our sakes. If it wasn't something Dad had asked for it was never going to work and I didn't want my last memories of Dad to be him telling me to f*** off again! I declined.

Although it didn't feel good saying no, I really believe if we had gone to pick him up he wouldn't have come with us, well not willingly anyway, and I couldn't bear the thought that he didn't want to be with us or to see the hurt in his eyes because he believed something totally untrue about me. No, it was better to say no, for all our sakes. Throughout all of this I wanted to keep the last memory of Dad and I being together while he was in hospital and him telling me when we should start building our little home at the back of his.

Chapter 10

THE FINAL FAREWELL

It was great being back home for a break, even if only for a short while. Well it was a break from work at least, obviously there was no break from how I felt about what was happening back in Ireland, and I wasn't alone in that. Poor Michelle was feeling the pressure so much, and mainly from Georgina that she even considered taking her kids out of school and moving over to Ireland. Now, how fair is that? A person feeling the pressure so much that they get to the point of considering disrupting their whole family and moving just to please others! Keith and I tried to help where we could by dealing with phone calls etc. and keeping in touch with the necessary people to make sure everything was going as best it could with Dad.

One of those we kept in contact with was the duty manager of Dad's carers who was a great support to us and would flag up any concerns that she had. She had recently been concerned that the support system was breaking down, which was leaving Dad vulnerable, and if this happened it would mean Dad going into a home! I was determined that was something that just wasn't going to happen one way or another. At this time we also became aware that not only wasn't Georgina happy with doing the rota, but her daily visits were becoming less and less. As I said earlier, she obviously had her reasons but I was struggling to get my head around all these changes with her. And why? And I still had some nagging thoughts about what had been said to Dad and others about us.

Quite often people who had been around Georgina had told me she had said certain things that just weren't true, and it was in one of the phone calls with the duty manager that she said, 'Not that I ever disbelieved Angela, but I now know Georgina had lied to Pete.' And my own niece said there were times when Georgina was making criticisms and accusations about me, even going to the length of criticising my mothering skills, that was until Michelle put her straight in no uncertain terms. Michelle told me that she couldn't help but think that she was trying to turn her against me, and it certainly looked like that from where I was standing. To be honest, when I was told this I couldn't be hurt anymore than I already had been but I was getting more and more angry.

Because of the concerns about Dad and his care we had started talking to the duty manager about the family taking back control instead of Georgina. After all we were going to be living there for quite a few months without returning to the UK, and even if I couldn't be in the front line looking after him I could at least be in the background doing my bit. This could take some time to organise and it had to be up to the health care service, but at least it was an option should things get any worse with Dad.

When I think back now that, 'break' in the UK definitely wasn't a break, the only difference was that I wasn't working, which I would actually have preferred. At least when I was with spirit I wouldn't be so consumed with all of this. Yep, about now a bit of avoidance would do me good, and thankfully moving over to Ireland was going to give me the avoidance I was looking for. I wasn't really enamoured with moving but I was looking forward to all that we had in store, especially in Wicklow Gaol. I just love walking into the place, and when you consider what it represented in the past such as hardship, tragedy, a hell hole where some battled to survive there and so many sadly lost their lives either because they were sentenced to death, or because they couldn't survive the awful conditions they were living in. For me, I always feel as though I'm being greeted by old friends on each investigation. I always meet a new one from the spirit world, and as crazy as this sounds I never feel pressure when doing investigations, they're either active or they're not, and compared to the story they have to tell when I connect with them about what they suffered in their life time, what I was going through was nothing compared to that.

Each story was different and each story represents heart break and anger, and boy oh boy can they show that when it gets active (especially the anger bit)! But you know what I've found is that it isn't only the prisoners that were incarcerated there but also the jailers in their own way. When they come forward and communicate their story can also be full of the hardship, guilt and sadness, and yes, some still feel the need to control but behind all that there is such sadness. In their own way they were imprisoned to their own emotions even though they are in spirit, and this can come through loud and clear in investigations. We meet quite a strange bunch in the gaol, soldiers, political rebels, men of the cloth... the list is endless, and each one of them gives us more knowledge and insight into what life was like back then.

It was business as usual as we settled into our new temporary home. So it was time to put a smile on my face and find the strength to carry on, most of the time acting like I didn't have a care in the world, and it really worked, well for a while at least. I couldn't avoid the pain too long as each phone call was giving out signals that Dad's health was failing fast. Some days the carers thought he was close to the end and then all of a sudden he would pick up again, not much, but he would come through the crisis time and time again. I always knew Dad was a strong man in his day, and even though he was dying and everything within him was closing down, his body wasn't going to give in without a fight. God he had some stamina, which is why it was so heartbreaking to see him be so ill and suffer so much. His suffering started the moment Mum passed over because a big part of him gave up then, and no matter how much support he had around him it just didn't make any difference. There were many family and friends who tried too hard to support him but now the only people he wanted around him were Georgina and her family.

I was replaced by another person. I was no longer his daughter and he wanted no more to do with me and he even went as far as crossing me off the list as his next of kin. Dad was very good at cutting people out of his life if they didn't live up to his expectations, and it was obvious that he really believed that I had 'betrayed' him, so I was no longer welcome in his life in any way, shape or form. Maybe to him Georgina was like the daughter he had always wanted. She was interested in farming, in fact she had her own farm, she was very much a country person, and I don't mean that derogatively, but he always used to tease me about being a 'townie' and not having a clue about animals, farms and horses etc. Dad had a great passion for horses and he used to talk endlessly about them and couldn't understand why I had no interest in them apart from thinking all animals are gorgeous. But what the heck did he expect? I was brought up in London for goodness sake! The only horses we used to see were those on a carousel when we went to the fair! You know, when I actually think about it I never really did live up to the expectations of others, including Mum and Dad.

Thankfully work was really busy and between the investigations and one-to-one readings I had very little time for thinking or wallowing in my own self pity and we certainly had plenty to concentrate on as it wouldn't be too long before our move over for a few months. As much as I loved our little cottage in Wicklow and it felt very homely, I wasn't really sure how I felt about staying there for a few months. There was a big part of me wanting to be close to Dad just in case we were needed, or should a miracle happen and he asked for me, but on the other hand I didn't want to leave my own home and my family and friends.

On a personal level this visit was very quiet and there wasn't a lot going on between Georgina and I except for a couple of texts I sent her reminding her that she needed to pull her finger out and organise Dad's care for the Christmas period. Again, there was no reply to my texts, but I had got used to that, and it didn't really bother me. The important thing was that she knew I would be keeping a close eye on how Dad's care was being organised.

The next couple of weeks in Ireland just flew by, we were now in the first week of December and it was time to return home and start organising Christmas. It was the 7th December when we left to go home and I can remember thinking as we came out of our front door that we'd be back before Christmas. I just knew it!

As nice as it was to be back home I couldn't really settle because Dad and the move we were making after Christmas was constantly on my mind. I know it was only for a few months, but it did bring up a lot of emotion in me, and I wasn't really handling any of it at all well. But I tried the best I could to get into the swing of things and get organised for the festive season. I was determined to make sure we had as good a time as we could under the circumstances. We had been home six days and I had had a couple of phone calls with the carers in that time and he wasn't doing too well at all.

On Saturday the 12th December we went away for the weekend to spend some time with our friends in Essex and have a bit of a break. We were having a lovely time and I was starting to relax a little. For the first time in months I felt like I had a bit of normality back. That is until I went to bed on the Sunday night and I had a visit from a gentleman spirit warning me to prepare for Dad's passing as he was on his way back to his spiritual home. I couldn't see his face, and I didn't recognise his energy, but I knew he wasn't a member of my family.

To this day I personally believe that he was a spirit guide coming through not only to warn me but to cushion the blow, and also to let me know that they were with me and were supporting me through this.

When I got up that morning Keith could see I was visibly shocked about something and asked me what was wrong. I turned around and said, 'I'm never going to see my dad alive again,' and then I broke down in tears. I felt so sick, and so scared! This was Monday 14th December at 8.30 am. Not long after I got a phone call from my niece to say that one of Dad's carers had phoned her and told her Dad had had a bad night, and they were in the process of having him taken into hospital again. I immediately phoned one of Dad's carers myself. Apparently he had had a good week but the evening before he started to go downhill and had a rough night, and they were waiting for the ambulance at that point. Her advice was to give it a couple of hours before I phoned again because they would need to settle him down. As luck would have it we had previously arranged to spend the Monday with our two nieces Sue and Michelle so we were already on our way to see them when all this was happening.

That morning we all just waffled on about anything really, just to take our minds off it all. I did contact the hospital at one stage but they were still settling him in, and I was told to call back later. By 1.30 pm I had had enough of waiting and not knowing how he was doing so I called the hospital again. It seemed to take ages to get through and then get transferred to his ward and when I eventually did get through and when the nurse realised I was his daughter she very gently said, 'I'm sorry to have to tell you but your Dad passed away 10 minutes ago.'

Keith, Sue and Michelle all knew by the shriek I made when I was told, and poor Keith had to take the phone from me because I couldn't take anything in. He was gone, and although I had been warned and had started preparing myself for this I just couldn't believe it, and all the preparing in the world doesn't soften the blow of knowing someone you love has passed. That pain in my stomach that comes with the tears was there once more. I think we can all relate to that pain and hurt of losing someone, the pain that is so unbearable, that feels like if we let it go we're never going to be able to survive the loss. This was worse than anything I could have possibly imagined. You see I felt as though I had lost Dad not once, but twice, the first time four months ago when this nightmare began, and now with his passing. I really didn't know how to pick myself up from this. All the while Dad was alive I had hope, but now that chance of a miracle had gone. Dad had passed without us making the peace, and he passed without me by his bedside.

Driving back to Dorset that night seemed to take forever even though I spent half the time on the phone letting people know. Now we were going to have to arrange the funeral, which wasn't going to be too difficult because Dad didn't want anyone at his funeral. This is something he had always been insistent on, and he didn't want a religious service because he was an atheist, and what was important now was to honour his last wishes. But we did go against him a little bit as there were friends and family who wanted to say their last goodbyes, and I needed that also. I had been denied being with him through his toughest time, I'm afraid I wasn't going to be denied this.

We set a date for people to pop along and pay their respects, and we also put a list together of all those who were welcome. Visiting Dad was by invitation only as I did not want Georgina or her family to visit him, and I made sure she got that message because I text her and told her to stay away – she was not welcome.

He had lost an incredible amount of weight and I barely recognised him. There was a comical moment when we decided to put his old hat and glasses on him. This hat was so old and holey and it had seen better days but he loved it. Now he was the dad we knew and loved. I may not have been at peace with all that had happened, but at least poor Dad was. He didn't deserve to suffer the way he did, and now at least he was at peace and on his way back to his 'spiritual home'.

We said our farewells to Dad on the 19th December, just six days before Christmas, always the worst time to lose anyone, but as we all know we just have to carry on, and considering what had happened we didn't do too badly, although when I look back now I realise I was just going through the motions. I can remember opening my pressies on Christmas morning with a smile that would have cracked if I moved my mouth, and although I tried to join in I couldn't get excited about anything. As far as I was concerned Christmas could do one! The move to Ireland was just a couple of weeks away now, and I so wanted to cancel now that Dad had gone, but we had made commitments and I wasn't going to let anyone down. And besides, we had to sort out Dad's house which was going to be a mammoth task because both Mum and Dad were hoarders.

It was really strange going back knowing that Dad was gone, and it was really weird to think we would be staying in one place for three months; no flitting back and forth to England for a while. Our poor little doggies Charlie and Snowey didn't know where the hell they lived!

We settled in really well and it was a bonus being so close to Mum and Dad's place so that we could sort things out. I know I've said this before about their place but the energy there was awful, but now it positively stung when you walked into it, especially in Dad's room. I know I was caught up in the middle of it all, which is why I would feel that way, but other's commented on it as well.

At first sorting the house out was hard work because I didn't want to let go of anything as everything seemed to have a memory to it. Even the teapot! But as time went on, it did get easier and I started to get used to the fact that it all had to go, and as always Keith and my family were so supportive, which really helped.

There was one day though when once again it all got to me and I felt so overwhelmed with all that had happened over the last few months. As I was sorting out Dad's things in his bedroom I could sense him around me. I just stood there remembering all the times I had brought him his tea and sometimes his dinner to him in bed when he wasn't up to much. I could remember all the little chats we used to have. Sometimes he would tell me a story of when he was a young man, and I would think, oh God, I don't know how many times I've heard all this. Oh, what I would give to hear those stories now. The only word I can use to describe how I felt at that time was devastation, and as I was clutching his clothes, sobbing my heart out, I fell to my knees saying, 'You did me so wrong, Dad, and you didn't even give me a chance. You did me so wrong.' I knew he was listening, and yes, I wanted him to know what I was going through and how I was suffering because of it all.

Some months later when I was on a mediumship course, we were placed in pairs and had to bring messages through from each other's loved ones in spirit. Well, my partner who I didn't know at all and until that day had never seen before, started to describe a gentleman she had with her and I knew immediately that it was my father. I did have a little laugh at this because he always said he 'didn't believe in all that rubbish', and yet here we were being reunited again. This wonderful medium started to give me a message from Dad and the words were, 'I did do you so wrong. I never gave you a chance and I'm so sorry.' Dad being sorry and admitting it, this was new! It was reach for the hanky time because the tears started falling and they wouldn't stop as hard as I tried. Dad knew the truth at last! This moment shall remain one of the most precious in my life and no one can take it away from me. I can't say it brought closure for me because the hurt was still raw at that time, but it really did help me to work toward it and help to start bringing some peace into my heart.

When I look back now I realise I had allowed all that happened over the last few months to strip me of my confidence, self-esteem, self worth etc. Many a time when cleaning my teeth in front of the mirror I would look at that person staring back at me and ask who the hell was she? Because I certainly didn't have a clue, and through all the smiles and laughs that I used to have, in reality deep down inside I felt like there was nothing left of me. I had always had very low confidence but I had worked hard with it, most of the time I felt pretty good about myself. Now, however, I seemed to be back to spending most of my time doubting myself on every level, including when I worked with spirit. Oh, I didn't doubt spirit at all, no it was just little old me that I doubted, and I would get so nervous when I was preparing to work with spirit and get myself into such a state because I felt so useless, that I would want to throw up. Of course I would never let anyone see how bad I really felt and spirit were marvellous as always, guiding and supporting me through it all. I find it incredible how quick we are to let the judgements and opinions of others take us down to such a low, dark level where it's so hard to see any light, and we just don't feel worthy of anything.

Once I got over the shock of losing Dad, and with the support of everyone in my life, I started to patch myself together again and Dad had given me another little piece of my self-worth back by giving me the gift of this wonderful message. Day by day my inner strength was getting stronger and for the first time in months I was looking forward to the future and being a part of life again. The clearing of Dad's house was going well and it wouldn't be too long before it went up for sale. We knew deep down that it wouldn't sell too quickly, although I personally hoped that it would, and I for one would be glad to see the back of it. Part of picking up the pieces was to decide what to do about the document we had built up about Dad, Georgina and defamation of character, the witnesses we had about certain events surrounding Dad and what we were told by those witnesses. Now, keep in mind that this document was built up not only from myself and my family's experiences, perceptions and also facts, but also from carers, and friend's experiences.

Keith and I did think long and hard about taking this situation to court, and to the press, and we would have been more than happy to give our account of what facts we had, but to do this we would also need to rely on other witnesses testimonies, and even though I know our niece would have been more than happy to speak out, my hunch was telling me that the other witnesses wouldn't be so willing, and before we went any further we needed to talk to them. As I thought no one was willing to stand up in court and give their account of what they had experienced, been told or had seen, and I know with one particular witness she was afraid of losing her job as she was one of his carers, and without them our case wouldn't stand so strong, so really the decision had been made for us that it was better not to go ahead with what potentially could be a very long, drawn out court case, and what would we really have gained from putting ourselves through that? It wasn't going to bring Dad back or change the last few months of his life, and I do believe that had we have carried on it would only have added to the heartbreak that I was already going through. Sometimes we have to realise if we can't change something in our life, then maybe we change the way we deal with it for our own sakes and allow ourselves to move on.

Was I angry? Yes, I was bloody angry, but not with those who felt they couldn't speak up; I could understand only too well why they wouldn't want to put themselves in a risky position with their jobs, after all they have got to earn a living to survive. But I was angry with the process that stopped them from being free to speak up. Just my view, but it felt like a gagging clause, and if that was the case, it's bloody ridiculous in this day and age. I know some people who felt we should risk it and go ahead, especially as apparently this wasn't the first time Georgina was in the centre of a situation very similar to this one and we were told by those involved in the case that the 'pattern of lies was identical' to what we had experienced. They were also very happy to tell us that she was 'the main benefactor of the will'. I stress here that this is only hearsay and I am not saying it as a fact, but if it's lies, then I wonder why would people want to lie about such a situation? Just a thought like! But in my view that situation was their axe to grind not ours.

For us it was time to take back control of our lives and find a way to finish the chapter, close the book and start looking ahead. At the end of the day my conscience is clear and I'm able to lay my head on my pillow and sleep at night.

This situation absolutely tore me apart and I felt like I was never going to pick up the pieces and put myself back together again. I had been stripped of my title and role as a daughter, which made me feel so unworthy and of no value. I really was not in a good place. Do I hate Georgina for what I believed she did to myself and my dad? Well hate is a strong word, but if I'm honest there were times when I really did hate the woman, but as time went on I realised she didn't deserve my energy because that would just keep me locked in a place of being her victim, and I am no one's victim. So I decided to forgive her and let her go, not for her, because she will have to live for the rest of her life with what she had done, but for me, because I wanted my life to carry on. She has to live her life knowing the part she played in this situation, and she had to answer to the consequences. I am a firm believer that what we put out there comes back to us in a karmic way, and let it be so.

This journey was a nightmare, but so much good has come out of it. Firstly, not a day goes by when I don't thank God for my wonderful family, for the thousands of blessings that I have in my life, and for life itself. I also realised that my most vulnerable point in my life was my strongest. No matter what was thrown at me I survived it; no matter what was taken away from me, I realised that my inner strength and spirit within could never be taken away from me. I never let go of my faith and my beliefs, in fact they strengthened. My appreciation for everything grew stronger and stronger day by day, especially for the love that I feel from and for my family. This situation opened my eyes for the very first time and I learned to appreciate the value of life, even through the toughest of times. I know this sounds so gushy, but it's so true.

For me it was onwards and upwards from now on.

Chapter 11

STARTING TO LIVE AGAIN

It's funny how life works. Just as we had decided to let go of the past and move on we met Tim Kelly, the founder of the Irish Ghost Hunters paranormal team, which helped us to focus on a new direction in life. Yep, you guessed it, we became part of the 'Ghost Hunting team'.

We were asked by the manager of the gaol to attend a private investigation that was being hosted there by Tim and his new team. We hit it off straight away and before we knew it we had joined forces. I remember those early days with such fondness. There were so many places in Ireland I had heard were 'haunted' and I was itching to get in there and investigate, and crazy or not one of the places that I wanted to visit was the infamous Hellfire Club way up in the Dublin mountains. I had heard so many stories about this place, none of them good and I wanted to find out for myself if they were true or just a myth, so one of our first investigations was going to be this derelict building way up high in a place that hasn't got a great reputation not only for its past but apparently stuff is still happening up there in this day and age. Exciting!

The Hellfire Club was originally a hunting lodge built by William Connolly. There are many legends connected to this place, one being that it was used as a den of iniquity and debauchery. The other legend that is so commonly known is that it's meant to be connected to the devil and apparently manifests there especially if you run around the building three times backwards. The two stories that I know of that connects it to the devil are: when they were building it they used stones from a burial site that is situated near there and apparently they even used a standing stone from this site as a lintel for the fireplace. Not long after it was built, a great storm blew the roof off and many believed it was the work of the devil for using materials from a sacred place. But of course the most popular legend is the one where a stranger turned up at the door of the Hellfire Club and was duly invited in for food and refreshments. Afterwards while playing cards one of the players dropped a card and stooped down to pick it up and noticed the stranger had a cloven hoof, and with that the stranger disappeared in a puff of smoke. Hmm... this story is the same story that's connected to Loftus Hall in Wexford, Ireland, and possibly other famous/infamous places around the country. So I needed to get up there and see for myself what I picked up, and I so wanted to meet the 'devil'!

The journey up there was an experience on its own. Situated right at the top of Montpelier Mountain it commands a beautiful view of the whole of Dublin, but getting up there is a bit of a pain as you have to park at the bottom of the mountain and walk up to it, which would normally take about 45/50 minutes, unless that is you get lost! And that's exactly what happened to us, and getting lost in the dark with the necessary equipment for an investigation and filming was a bit of a nightmare, and it was really spooky! With every step we took I could feel the energy changing around us. The woods that we had to walk through held a lot of secrets both past and present, it was eerie, and although I could sense spirit around us, to be honest I was more concerned about who we may meet that was living! It took us two hours before we finally reached there. We were knackered, but relieved we made it. We were being watched by spirit, I just knew it. And the closer we got to the building the stronger the sensation, and the more I felt it was a warning to stay away, but now we had come this far we certainly weren't going to turn back.

What a foreboding building, and even though it was derelict the atmosphere was awful! As we walked through it from room to room there was a very clear picture forming of just what this place was used for. It was a 'gentleman's club' and I use the word 'gentleman' very lightly. This was indeed a place where a lot of drinking, gambling and from what I was picking up abuse went on in days gone by. The energy there was so negative and strong, which doesn't surprise me really because it's known that people still go up there even now to practice dark arts and the occult. There was one room at the end of the building that we believe was a kitchen at one stage, and as we walked in I immediately sensed two gentlemen around us, both with a very strong presence and warning me to keep clear because they didn't want me to discover their little secrets. Our K2 metres were going ballistic and even though it was cold the temperatures kept changing around us. These two gentlemen were frequent visitors to this den when they were alive, and were still happy to visit, even though they had passed over, to keep control of all that still goes on within those walls. But they weren't whom I was focussing on at that time because there was the most beautiful young spirit girl that had joined us, and if my memory serves me correctly she was aged between 16 to 18 years old. The emotions I was feeling from her were so strong and overwhelming, and as I was connecting with her I became so aware of just how much she had suffered in her brief lifetime. As I was telling the group about her and pointing to the spot she was standing the K2 meters went crazy. Her name was Rosie and she had been abused by those who frequented this God forsaken place. She had worked there and sadly was used as more than just a servant. I felt so overwhelmed by what she was giving me and to the surprise of myself and the group I broke down in tears because it had affected me so much. But as always, I didn't want the team just to take my word for it so I asked Rosie to answer our questions through the K2 meters by lighting them up every time the answer was yes, and that's exactly what she did. We could all feel the emotion from what she endured building up around us as we heard her story. Were these two gentlemen that insisted on staying so close to us anything to do with her abuse? Well let's put it this way, they were definitely aware of it and my opinion is that yes, they were.

Right through the night we had activity one way or another, from changes of temperatures to team member emotions being affected, or feeling like they were being touched. It was a night to keep on our toes because anything could happen. At one point we were on the first floor chatting away when all of a sudden one of our team members started to look spaced out, and her eyes started rolling like she was just about to pass out, there was nothing coming from her, not even when we called her name to bring her forward, and yet five minutes earlier she was fine. She was standing by an open gap that used to be a window so for a few seconds it was pretty scary and we needed to make sure we got her away from that area pretty quickly. Thankfully once we got her out of that room she was back to her normal self. Something happened in every room we went in. People hearing footsteps, that knowing feeling that we were being watched, being touched etc., so all in all a good investigation, but it wasn't over yet.

Keith and Tim decided to take a walk through the woods that are behind the building. I personally thought they were off their trolleys! God knows what they could encounter from the living, let alone the dead, but off they went with torches and camcorder in hand while the rest of us stayed behind to carry on with the investigation. After about 10-15 minutes the energy around us lifted and for the first time since we got there all felt really calm. Whatever spirit we had had around us that night had decided to leave us, which I think we were all relieved about because we were all so exhausted and just wanted our beds now. All we had to do was wait for Keith and Tim to return, and when they did they seemed pretty pleased with themselves as they had a lot of activity on their walk around, and when Tim reviewed the footage on his camcorder they had captured a bright white shining light floating past them just as Tim says, 'What's that?' They had heard footsteps out there and it definitely wasn't any of us, as the rest of us stayed together in a group while they were gone. It could have been an animal, or even someone playing the fool, but it is strange that it coincided with Tim getting this footage, and it's also strange that as they left the group and went out on their own, all the activity inside the building up and left us too! This investigation was awesome and I consider us to be very lucky to meet the spirits that were connected to that depressing place. Even if they did try to freak us out at times.

This was the first of four investigations that we ended up doing at the Hellfire Club, each time meeting with new and old spirit who never let us down showing us what they can do, and I believe there are still many more spirit to meet there, but not for me as I've had my fill of the infamous Hellfire Club. We had gone along and heard the stories of poor Rosie and the other gentlemen, we felt the emotions, heartbreak and anger that was in the hearts of those who walked that dreadful place a long time ago and we had touched on the secrets that still live on within those walls. Did it live up to my expectations? Yes, it did, although I didn't meet the devil, but then I didn't really expect to. If he exists and if he resides there he obviously didn't want to meet us that night, or any of the other nights we've visited there. I do however believe we met with the evil behaviours that resided in the hearts of those who hid behind the grandeur of who they were and who they mixed with back then. I also can't help but wonder how often the energy in this building is affected by those who visit there to practice dark arts and the occult in this day and age. It's not uncommon to hear of people going up there to practice the dark arts and some of the time just for the fun of it. I truly hope they know what they're doing because playing with the occult when you don't have a clue what you're doing can bring on many problems, and it definitely shouldn't be practiced just for the fun of it. The thing with investigations is that you never know who you're going to connect with, or from what walk of life they came from, but I have to say, as long as you respect spirit then spirit will respect you.

Some people ask if I ever get scared when doing an investigation. I can honestly say I have never been scared of spirit or what they can do, but I have however been very scared of the living and what some people are capable of. As we all know there are some people on this earth that are far more capable of doing us harm than spirit ever could. Having said that, there has been the odd occasion after doing an investigation that I have got slightly worried that spirit may choose to get their own back on me if I've had to go back into an area where we've been working that night, especially if it's been pretty active and I've pushed my luck with them a bit.

I still laugh at a memory I have of a castle we were investigating. It had been lively and I met with a spirit that didn't take a shine to me from the start. At the end of the séance I had to go from one part of the castle to the other mainly in the dark, which I didn't relish, and felt very uneasy. As I approached the kitchen area I had that awful feeling that someone was behind me and was getting closer and I could hear loud footsteps. I knew it wasn't any of the team members and I was bricking it! My mind was working overtime; what if it was that gentleman spirit I had upset? What was he going to do? OMG! I had taken myself down every road that I possibly could to put the fear of God into myself. My knees were trembling, my heart was racing and I was praying that I make it to the kitchen without anything happening. And then all of a sudden, I heard gentle footsteps behind me, completely different to the ones I had heard just a few seconds earlier, and they were approaching very fast. In the end curiosity got the better of me and I turned around only to find the most beautiful German shepherd running towards me. He was gorgeous and so friendly and we walked together to the kitchen. I can remember feeling so secure with him by my side, and although the feeling of being watched was still there it wasn't as severe. By the time I got to the kitchen I was so relieved and felt a little stupid as well. Fancy getting myself into that state; me, an experienced medium and investigator! When the lady who organises the investigations and looked after us saw that I had the family dog by my side she was so surprised and told me, 'He never does that; he always stays upstairs with the family when investigations are going on.' So why did he come down that night, and in particular why at that particular time? Was it to protect me? And to add to the intrigue of this story, whilst we were in the kitchen we all heard footsteps outside running past the kitchen and followed them with great speed, and guess what, no one was there!

I'm a strong believer that animals are psychic and can sense danger long before we can. They're smart cookies and so faithful as well, and I'm convinced if that beautiful doggie didn't walk by my side that night, something was going to happen, I'm not sure what, but I do know that gentleman spirit would have tried to have made his point known. And of course I didn't help myself by feeding my fears and allowing them to get out of all proportion, and I should have known only too well fear is not a feeling we should let loose at these times, or in our everyday life for that matter. The minute we let loose all our fears we're no longer grounded and can create situations that are more harm than good, like stress and anxiety for example, and I bet you can all relate to that. Fear can be our greatest friend when we're truly in a life threatening situation, it keeps us safe and brings out our survival instincts when needed. But fear can also be our greatest enemy when it's not founded or realistic and can bring out the worse side of us.

So, we've done investigations in castles, derelict buildings, graveyards, gaols, ghost villages, airfields, pubs, woods, churches, fields and many more, and I have enjoyed each and every one of them. But it's all very well going into these kind of places and connecting with spirit, asking them to do stuff and at the end of the night saying 'Thank you very much and goodbye,' but not all paranormal activities take place in old 'haunted' places. What about the people experiencing paranormal activity in their homes? And believe me, there are more than you think that are in this situation. I just love to get my teeth into investigating a private family residence because they're very different. For a start it's normally warmer and I'm not freezing my toes off for a change! When a family is having activity in their home it can have a huge affect on their everyday life and normally by the time we're called in things are getting pretty desperate. We normally find at this point that first and foremost they're looking for someone to confirm to them that they're not going crazy and that what's happening is real. When activity is happening in our own space it can be quite frightening and if the activity is frequent and depending on the strength of the activity, the family can be sleep deprived, becoming anxious and really don't want to be in their own home because it no longer feels theirs, or safe for that matter. Although not in all cases, but certainly in some occasions the activity has even affected the relationships within the family unit. So yeah by the time we meet them they can be pretty desperate and just want it all to come to an end.

But as I said earlier, not everyone feels that way. Some people can handle it far better than others and I have found in many cases that those who are not so freaked out by what's going on are those who have a healthy belief in the spiritual side of life. What I mean by that is that they have a greater understanding that spirit are just wanting to let them know that they are there and are trying to get their attention. They stay grounded and they realise it's not a question of 'getting rid of spirit' but more about spirit needing healing to help them pass over. But of course regardless of whether they are freaking out or staying grounded the investigation is just the beginning. Some people think that we're going to come in, gain evidence to prove they're right, pass them over and then all will be hunky dory. If only! Remember, spirit were there before we ever were and who are we to decide whether they should go or not? And let me tell you, if spirit do not want to go they won't! Well at least not without a fight and a lot of persuading as the past experiences we've had have proved.

There was one particular case that stands out where there was more than one spirit in the home. A lovely lady called Julie was having a lot of activity in her home. Her TV would turn itself up to full volume while they were watching it, at the same time things started to move across the room, and although no one was using the phone, all of a sudden they would hear a man's voice coming from it, and the two youngest children being woken up in the middle of the night by spirit sitting on the end of their bed, and these are just a few of the things they would encounter regularly. A male named William, two females (one young, one elderly) and an adorable little boy were present, and each spirit was grabbing the attention of the family in different ways. The older of the two females just wanted to watch over the family just as she would have her own when she was alive. The young girl was only about 17 years old, named Lucy and enjoyed being around the teenage girl that lived there and very often made her presence known to her in her bedroom, but the problem was that she would do it in the middle of the night a lot of the time. But the man, well, he was a completely different kettle of fish! He was determined to stay in control by way of being loud and walking up and down the hallway day and night, and I believe he was the culprit of most of the other stuff that had been going on. He was angry and was showing it through his strength of sound. What an investigation that turned out to be! As soon as we started this gorgeous little boy came through. Adam was his name. Bless him, he just wanted to be around younger children and be a part of their family. He was lost and looking for his own family. He was so lovely to work with and happily crossed over to be with his family with the agreement that he was welcome to come back and visit anytime he wanted.

When William came through it was a very different story. He wasn't going anywhere and was very forceful in letting us know it. As we worked with him through a séance and as he was drawing closer we were all feeling apprehensive and we were right to be. Things started to get quite active very quickly and I could sense that it was going to be hard to keep control of the situation. How right I was, because in no time at all things took a turn for the worse! Julie, the owner of the property started to shake uncontrollably, although I told her it was best if she left the séance and go through and sit with Keith but she didn't want to, which I understand because Julie is a lot like me and doesn't like giving in to anything, but it did mean I had to be extra vigilant with what was happening. The energy was getting stronger and stronger and everyone could see how Julie was being affected as her whole body was now shaking uncontrollably, her face changed totally which was quite concerning for all of us, but before I had chance to do anything I heard a man's voice coming from her mouth. It was deep, husky and spine chillingly eerie.

This was my first experience of what some may call a 'possession'. I personally don't know what to call it, but I do know it was bloody scary, even for me. I immediately called Keith and got him to take her out of the room so that he could bring her forward and bring her back down to earth. Meanwhile back at the table we were desperately trying to pass William into the light. This was one spirit that needed a lot of healing and the only way for that to happen was by helping him pass into the light, but it wasn't going to be easy. In normal circumstances I wouldn't be so insistent but when spirit is capable of creating so much chaos it's time for them to go, especially now that we had been there as he was a tad upset that we had been called in and could take it out on the family, so all in all it was better if he wasn't around. Don't get me wrong, he wasn't banished totally, he could still come back and visit but he wouldn't be able to control the household anymore. Thankfully and eventually we were able to persuade him to leave and when he did we just all collapsed back in our chairs and took the deepest and biggest breath with relief. At this point Keith walked back into the room and said, 'He's gone hasn't he?' and went on to explain that bringing her back to normal had been proving difficult and each time he thought he had calmed her down within seconds she was shaking from head to foot again, and then calming down again.

The pattern that Keith was describing matched what was happening with us. One minute he would calm down and I thought he was so close to crossing over, then he would flare up and get lively again and when he did finally cross over not only did it get calm with us but also where Keith and Julie were. Two separate rooms and yet what was happening in one room was matching what was happening in the other room with Julie and Keith. Now I found that amazing. Although it was a tough investigation it was exciting, and we all experienced something we had never experienced before, but our work doesn't stop there. The psychological effects from having spirit visitors can be great for some but it may be hard for some people to believe that the activity has stopped and spirit has gone. Some remain fearful that it could come back, unfortunately unable to let go which could create problems on its own as a build up of fear is an energy that spirit can feed off. But not only that, it can create a negative atmosphere around a person, and believe me, that can be just as nasty, which is why Keith and I like to continue to keep in touch to continue working with the families trying to put their minds at ease wherever we can.

In many cases one investigation is enough to settle down the visits and activity that's been going on, but not in all cases. Very often we have to return and hold a second investigation and when this happens it's my view that it's nothing sinister, it just means that more healing is needed within spirit for them to cross over and be at peace. They can return quite a few times before full healing finally takes place.

Anyway, back to our investigation. Julie only wanted William to go as he was the one that was causing the trouble. Josie and Lucy were welcome to stay, and as I said before, little Adam was welcome to visit anytime he liked. We did have a lovely séance with both the ladies, and they were so lovely to work with. They were both connected to the land, but not related to each other, they were aware of each other's presence and were quite happy to share the current family with each other. The only condition that we had was that Lucy didn't keep Anita awake at night, and she has kept her word. I also have to say Julie and her family were absolutely wonderful to work with, and made us feel so welcome, and since doing the investigations we have become good friends with her and her family.

Although not all investigations are as extreme as this one, it does give a good insight into what can happen and the effects it has on a family unit.

Give me private investigations any day; they're so much more rewarding.

Chapter 12

PICKING UP THE PIECES

Keeping busy with my mediumship demonstrations, readings and working with Irish Ghost Hunters was helping me to deal with the pain of all that had happened, and for the first time in ages I was getting up in the morning without dreading what the day would bring. I was learning how to laugh again and I was starting to feel like I was part of all who were around me. I was finally picking up the pieces and getting my life back and it felt good! Don't get me wrong, not a day went by when I didn't think of Dad, or Georgina for that matter, which naturally brought up all the hurt again, but staying in that place and feeling sorry for myself wasn't going to bring Dad back, change the past or help me move forward. Yes, my emotions were all over the place, and yes, I felt like I had a huge mountain to climb, but if I just took one step a day it was one step away from all that crap and taking me one step closer to feeling like my old self again. But what was really getting to me the most, and without realising it at the time, I was bloody angry with myself for not listening to my gut hunch about this woman. Why? Oh why?

On reflection I can see now that I didn't want to rock the boat. The minute I met her I didn't take to her and I certainly didn't trust her, but she was Mum and Dad's friend not mine, and to be honest I thought that it was me being jealous of her. It felt like she could do no wrong, especially with Dad. If I have any regrets about the way I handled it, it's that I never listened to all the warnings my intuition was giving me; that gut feel that I had every time she was around, and I do sometimes wonder if things would have been different if I had been prepared to act on what my gut was saying. What I'm really trying to say here, and you've probably heard it a thousand times before, but I can't stress enough how important it is to listen to what our gut has to say about the different situations in life, that psychic ability that will keep you on the straight and narrow.

Yes, we're all psychic to some degree or another, and yes, that even means you! Don't be surprised by that statement; why should you be any different? To those of you who don't see in themselves that we all really do have the ability to tune into all that's going on around us at all times, you just need to learn how to develop these abilities. We may all be very different and very unique in so many ways but for all that, we all have the same ability to develop and fine tune our psychic abilities.

I bet you've all walked into a room where you just know something has happened there and you can cut the atmosphere with a knife, or you have walked into a building and felt certain emotions that you didn't feel before entering. That's you tuning in and using your psychic abilities. You're picking up on the layers and the vibrations of the energy that's been left behind. Think of it this way, everywhere you go you leave a piece of you behind in energy form. Every piece of land and every building has many layers of energy from the different eras and the different events that took place there, and of those who have lived or walked in days gone by. And believe it or not, you can walk in and connect with those different layers to help give you a bigger picture of all that's gone before. How amazing is that! You may be in the present but for that brief time you experience the past with all the feelings and emotions that's connected to it! And the same can be said of people. All of us at some stage or another will meet someone and you instantly know what they've been through, what they're going through at that time, and yes, you may even get an idea of what may happen, and nine times out of ten you would be right.

So how do we get all this information? Through our senses (sight, sound, feel, taste, smell and intuition), and these senses are working for us all of the time even though we're not aware of it, and it's through our senses that we learn how to perceive the world. A good way to find out what your dominant sense is, is to sit back and think for a moment and ask yourself how you perceive your world? When you think of past experiences do you see pictures? Is it like a film running in your mind? You might want to also think ahead to something you're planning in the future – is it in pictures, or again like a film running? If so you are visual, so life to you will be run like a movie in your mind. Or when thinking of situations do you hear voices talking things through with you when you're trying to sort something out? (No I don't mean the kind they would have you sectioned for!) Or when you think back to past experiences do you remember every word that was said? And when looking to the future do you have a chat with yourself on how it's going to be? If the answer is yes to all of these then you are auditory, so life will be a bit like a book, where all the different experiences you have is a chapter in a book. Does something have to feel right with you before you make a decision? Do your feelings do a flip when thinking back to past experiences? What about when you're looking to the future, do you feel what it's going to be like? If so you're kinaesthetic. Being kinaesthetic means that you're very much a feeling person in most situations, so your feelings are your dominant sense. Now, visual, auditory and kinaesthetic and all of your other senses (gustatory, which is your sense of taste, olfactory which is your sense of smell and your intuition) will work in partnership with them, and they're all as important as each other, especially your intuition. So your senses are like your antenna for picking up all the info you need to tune into people, places and challenging situations, etc. So, that's how we pick things up, but where does all this wonderful info come from?

Every one of us has an energy field around us called our aura, and there are many different layers to this aura but we're going to focus on the seven main layers. Each layer of our aura is connected to the main energy centre that we have flowing through our body called our chakras. Each chakra and each layer of our aura relates to our physical, emotional, mental, and spiritual well-being and if we're not balancing life well or we have a lot of stress, challenges, worries etc. this will knock our chakra's out of sync and will show in our aura. There are some who can actually see the different colours that flow throughout our aura, but don't get too hooked up on this, not everyone has this ability and to be honest you don't really need to because when you tune into someone's aura you will get a sense of knowing what's going on in their life. There are some really great books on this subject if you want to gain more knowledge. There is so much we can learn about a person through their aura. Their health, their mental and emotional state, and their spiritual growth are just a few things that will become clearer to you as you work with them. Practice it with friends and family, you would be surprised what comes up.

When people come to me for a reading I am very often asked to do a psychic reading only as not everyone wants to connect for a message from spirit, they're just curious about their present and their future and so often they are surprised by the accuracy of the reading and yet it's nothing mysterious or supernatural to be able to give a reading, it's just a question of tuning into your sitter's energy. And it's not just us humans that have an energy field, every object that has ever been created is created from energy so it is possible to tune into anything. For example, hold a ring that belongs to a friend or an acquaintance and see what information you receive from it, and I can guarantee it won't only be the stuff you know about them. Yep, when you tune into the different layers of the aura and the frequency it holds you gain an insight into the lives of others. But my friends if you intend to practice this, please get the person's permission first. Although we're receiving info all the time on those around us, it's a very different thing if someone is intending to tune into a person in order to get a deeper level of information.

Of course having a deeper understanding of energy fields and developing your psychic abilities is great for paranormal investigations, and don't think you need to have a medium with you because you don't, you don't really even need scientific equipment either, you just need your senses and an understanding of how to tune it. Simples! I do have to say though it's a lot more fun when you mix the psychic, science and mediumship together. Just think of the evidence you can accumulate when all three tally, and they very often do!

You will find, regardless of whether you want to join the spooky world of the paranormal or you just want to have a better quality of life, of being able to open up and gain a greater understanding of how you perceive your world, receive the messages from your environment and those around you, by developing your psychic abilities and fine tuning your senses really does create a better perspective and even a better way of dealing with life. Now, there's a thought! A better way to live! Finding a better way to deal with situations and developing a new awareness of how we make life so much more complicated for ourselves than it really needs to be really is possible, not easy, but possible.

So how do we do this and make the impossible possible? By getting to know yourself better, by becoming your own best friend and learning to trust in yourself. Yes, I know you've heard it all before a thousand times, and there are many books out there on this subject and probably each and every one of them is very well worth reading so I'm not going to add another one to the collection. Instead I'm going to share with you how I started on my path of change.

How many of us truly know ourselves? I mean truly know, how and what makes us tick? What our beliefs are? I know that for most of my life I didn't have a clue, which is why I struggled so often in my earlier life. I was an anxious kind of person with a lot of fears and phobias and I believe all of this contributed to my breakdown. I was also very much a people pleaser, which to be honest nearly always backfired on me and I normally ended up upsetting someone somewhere. Well you know that saying, 'you can't please all of the people all of the time'? How true! Deep down I was always a goodhearted soul, but the problem was I never saw that in myself, I just saw the wreck of a person that I felt inside, and although I had overcome a lot as I worked through my breakdown, I still had no trust in life, and I certainly didn't have any trust in anyone else, or myself for that matter. Whenever there was a chance of life getting better or if I saw that my luck was starting to change and my dreams were within reaching distance I would hear this little voice (don't worry it wasn't the kind of voice you hear when you're losing the plot!) saying to me, *Don't be stupid, you don't deserve that. People like you don't get those chances.* At the time this little voice was strong, powerful and very corrosive and each time I heard it, it would chip away another little piece of the little bit of self-worth I had.

Think about it for a moment. When you're aiming for something that you're dreaming of, do you hear a voice of encouragement, or do you hear a voice telling you you're worthless? If it's the latter just close your eyes for a moment and listen to that voice; whose voice is it? Because one thing's for sure, it's definitely not yours! It's a voice from the past, a voice that would give you a lecture every time you did something wrong, or they perceived that you had done something wrong. We all deserve to be happy and we all deserve to have our dreams fulfilled, but the problem is so many of us spend a lot of time searching for the one thing that's going to make us happy, but a lot of the time we struggle to find what we're looking for because we haven't got a clue what it is that would really make us happy because we're too busy listening to that little voice bringing us down. Is it any wonder we become so closed off to all that's possible? Is it any wonder we learn to think within the box instead of braving it out there in a world that gives us so many opportunities because it can be too scary otherwise?

There's not a day goes by when I don't reflect on the screwed up person I was and how different life used to be for me, and the way it is now. I know luck plays a part in it but it's not all about luck – our thoughts, beliefs, and actions definitely play a part. I saw myself as useless, feisty and unlovable, and because of that, life wasn't going to be anything other than turbulent! I spent most of my early years jumping from one crisis to another being angry and defensive, which inevitably pushed friends and family away and pushed me over the edge. I was permanently angry, and it was also the one emotion that was safe to use in our house because it was really the one emotion that was used, understood and accepted, and boy did I do anger well! I don't think any of us enjoyed behaving that way, we were just used to it, and it kept us safe because nothing makes a person more vulnerable than to have their feelings dismissed. God, I gave everyone around me a really hard time when I went into one, and I always went straight into the defensive. 'There's no talking to you' is a phrase I was very used to hearing. Of course behaving like that didn't resolve any problems, all it ever created was more crap to add to my emotional baggage, which in turn would turn the next situation into a drama because of all my pent up feelings.

So why would I behave like that? Well, I think the main reason is because I was so frightened of getting it all wrong. I always felt wrong in every aspect and I used to look at others wishing that I had their sense, their strength, their capabilities, and as I write this I still feel really sad that I spent so many years believing the worst about myself. What a waste of time and of life! So how did I learn to think, feel and behave this way? As much as I loved my mum and I know she loved us kids, her way of dealing with any challenges or problems was identical. She could lose her temper very, very quickly and whoever was around her at the time would need to find a quick escape route, otherwise they would end up somehow being blamed for something. Bless her, she did get herself into a state over the smallest of things and end up losing the plot but solving nothing. Do you see the pattern forming? My reactions to life were carbon copies of how Mum dealt with things. I also learned very quickly that being angry and defensive was a great survival technique.

Oh, there were many survival techniques I learned as a kid that kept me emotionally safe. On the surface I was arrogant, confident and cocky but deep down I was insecure, scared and really quite lonely, but I wasn't going to show that. People kept their distance and although I was lonely that suited me because I had very little trust in people or in myself for that matter, and on a subconscious level I honestly didn't believe that I deserved to have good in my life.

Never underestimate the power of your thoughts my friends. What you don't allow to make you can break you. We have so many opportunities in life but the way we think can send us into a very negative spiral. I was one of those people that constantly erred on the negative side of life in my younger days; I managed to attract the wrong kind of people into my life constantly. People that would use me, abuse me create dramas then walk away leaving me to pick up the pieces. Of course not everyone that came into my life was like that, but as I said earlier I had a knack of making sure people didn't stay around too long, all except Keith that is. From the moment I met him I knew he was the one for me. He was the one I wanted to let in and thankfully he had the ability to see behind the facade I put on. He saw the vulnerable side of me, the real me. Don't get me wrong it was by no means an easy ride for him especially when I tested him to the limits. I know all this sounds cheesy, but it's the truth when I say Keith helped show me the way forward, he showed me there was another way to live life other than argue all the time. He gave me the stability I needed to let go of all that had held me back. Sounds simple to 'let go' but I think we all know it's easier said than done.

Over the years, with Keith holding my hand and supporting me I learned to unravel all the crap that I had created, that had been so intricately woven throughout my life and by the time I reached my 30s and with the help of Keith and not forgetting all the counselling sessions, I had come a long way and for a short while I thought I had dealt with all that was there, that all the pain had gone and the past was well and truly buried. So I couldn't understand why I would get so far in life then something would happen and it didn't have to be anything major, in fact it could be something and nothing but it would catapult me straight back to my early years, with all the painful memories and the painful feelings and emotions that were attached to them. All the experiences I had had in life were still creating strong emotions, fears and anxieties in my present life. It felt like I was living on a permanent roller coaster with no chance of getting off.

It's funny how things come into your life just at the right time. I Can't remember how it came about but in the late 90s I had started to hear about the concept of the 'inner child' we all have within us and how damaged he/she can become through life's experiences, creating unhealthy thought's, behaviour's and beliefs. This sounded right up my alley and just what I needed, so I promptly signed up for the 10 week course. Little did I realise at that time I would be so positively affected by the changes in me as I started to understand why I was the way I was and where it all stemmed from that I signed up for the second and the third course. I was hungry to know more. I wanted to know just how I felt as a child and how I could make all that pain go away now. It really was mind blowing , and yes sometimes I felt like I had been dragged through a hedge backwards, and very often the tears would flow like a tap that had been left to run constantly, which made a difference to the tap that had been slowly and constantly dripping on my forehead for years. Yep, the tears may have been falling, but I was starting to find an inner peace and a deeper understanding of why I kept being pulled back by my past.

But I didn't want to stop there. If all of this new awareness coupled with the new tools and techniques that I was using could help me, it would do the same for others and I wanted to help others and be a part of that healing process.

My path was set, I wanted to train as a psychotherapist.

Chapter 13

A Lesson in Forgiveness

I spent many years working as a psychotherapist, and I have to say it was a privilege to be a part of someone's personal growth. To watch someone learn to value themselves, recognise their own self-worth and find the strength and courage to carry on and overcome all the obstacles they have to face is so beautiful and rewarding. But of course not all cases had the 'happy ending' and there were times when I wanted so much to see a client challenge and overcome their battles but they couldn't quite do it. Sadly their destructive patterns of life continued. But you know just because they couldn't quite move forward and win their war doesn't make them weak, it just means they weren't ready at that point and maybe they never will be, but I never stop hoping that somehow, someway they will find the strength and courage they need to work towards a new life, a new pattern. At that time I could never imagine having any other profession in life, until that is I started to work with spirit.

In the early days of my mediumistic development it wasn't too bad, but as time went on spirit had a habit of turning up everywhere and anywhere including in therapy sessions with clients, and as much as it was great having spirit so near, it wasn't very useful when I was trying to concentrate on my client. I hadn't learned how to control when I was open to working with them and when I wasn't. Very often I would find myself sitting with a client and their mum and dad, Uncle Joe or Aunty Fanny would pop in to say hello, and it was tougher still when the client was seeing me for grief counselling and the person they had loved and lost was right next to them. Oh, it was heart-warming for me to see them still so close to their loved one, but sadly I couldn't share this with the client as it wouldn't be considered ethical. There was a line I couldn't cross from being a therapist to being a medium. Oh, if only I could have told them. I believe it would have given them great comfort and maybe help to bring closure for them. I know it would have for me when I was grieving.

In the early stages of my mediumistic development I was all over the place and it took a while before I got it under control. I laugh now when I look back and recall some of the experiences I had with them. I would walk into a room and sense spirit, I would wake up in the middle of the night only to hear my name being called and low and behold I would see spirit standing over me wanting me to give a message to someone and there was one night I remember when I was woken up but at that point I wasn't sure why. After a few minutes I got up to go to the loo, as one does, and as I walked towards the door I walked straight into what I can only describe as an energy field. 'Oh, I'm so sorry,' I exclaimed as I bounced back and realised there was a gentleman spirit who had popped into say hello. Whilst sitting on the loo I remember thinking, hang on a minute, this ain't on! I'm tired and I need my sleep without being interrupted. As I walked back into the bedroom the gentleman was still there so I walked up to him and said, 'As much as I would love to stop and have a chat with you I'm really tired and I want to sleep. Can you come back tomorrow and we can talk then?' I'm ashamed now to think I did that! Spirit have given me so much and I treat them like that. Not on really but I know they've forgiven me.

Another time I was sitting on a tube on the Bakerloo line happily reading my book when I looked up and across the carriage and there was a gentleman spirit opposite me, not saying anything just staring at me. What was great about this though was literally a few weeks later there was a documentary on the television about tubes and their 'ghosts' and to my joy the gentleman I saw was mentioned and had in fact been seen by others on many occasions.

All of this was really exciting but it was also exhausting, and as much as I wanted to work with spirit I also wanted some normality in my life. I had started to feel as though 'normal' didn't exist anymore. Now that may seem ungrateful and a bit like I'm looking a gift horse in the mouth because after all I had been wanting all of these kind of experiences to happen for so long and have a closer link with spirit, and now here I was saying 'I want normal,' but spirit knew what I meant. They knew I wasn't being ungrateful, they knew I just needed some support and guidance on how to control when and where I work. After all, us mediums still have the stresses, strains and challenges of life. We still have family crises and tragedies just like everyone else and spirit understand that better than anyone else. If we're going to be ambassadors for spirit we need to be able to have both our feet in this world and not one foot here in the physical and one foot in the spirit world, otherwise we've got no chance of sorting out the problems and challenges that land in our path, otherwise we can't do our best for spirit. Thankfully my spirit guides helped me to find that happy medium (pardon the pun). So clocking off and having a normal life is part of working for spirit.

Having said all that there are times when I've clocked off and spirit want me to do some overtime and in those situations I'm happy to clock on again, like the time we were invited to a party. I only knew a handful of people there, but as soon as I walked into the restaurant where the party was being held I was immediately aware of spirit with me. She was a lovely lady and I know she would have been big and bouncy when she was here on earth and she wasn't any different in spirit. She told me she wanted to get a message to her daughter and promptly showed me who she was as she went straight by her side. Hmm, easier said than done in the middle of a dinner party! But somehow I was going to have to find the way. How the hell was I going to fix it so that I could start chatting to her? I mean I can't just walk up to her and say,

'Hello, my name's Angie, I'm a medium and I've got your mother with me.' She's gonna think I've escaped from the funny farm! And somehow I also had to find out if she was drinking because I never give readings to anyone who has a few drinks inside them. I've always been taught that 'spirits and spirits don't mix', and I totally agree with that. Emotions can do funny things to us when we've had a few drinks and we can become over emotional, angry, sad, etc. It's actually very hard to know how a person is going to react with a drink inside them, and besides anything else they may not even remember the message the next day, which would be such a shame.

First things first though, I needed somehow to get chatting to the daughter of this lovely spirit lady. I made my way towards the bar when she was standing with her husband. As I approached I was lucky enough to hear her say, 'I'll have another orange juice,' as her husband ordered their next round. Phew, that's a blessing, she's not drinking. Now all I had to do was strike up a conversation. I got to the point when I thought, what the heck, in for a penny in for a pound! I'm just gonna go for it! I turned to her, smiled and said, 'It's a good turnout for Stan's Birthday; you here for his party too?' Damn – not a very original way to start a conversation. I felt so stupid when it was clear that most of the people there were there for the party, but it was the only thing I could think of, and it worked! Before long we were exchanging names. 'My name's Angie,' but I omitted the medium part. For the sake of anonymity let's call this lady Bella. I could see Bella was such a gentle soul and very friendly, so it was easy to be in her company, but it still wasn't going to be easy. I must admit I felt a bit of a stalker hanging around her like a bee around a honey pot and wondered if I should just come straight out and tell her I had got a message from her mum, but just as I was about to dive in we were told to sit in our places at the table. I told Keith I had to sit next to her and explained why and thankfully between the pair of us we managed it.

Luckily we had a couple of things in common, one of them being that she was Irish as were my family, and of course I work extensively in Ireland so I used this as a common ground to talk about my mum and where she was from, that she had passed and how much I missed her. Bingo! 'I know how you feel,' she said. 'My mum died four years ago and I miss her terrible.'

I could see the emotion in her as she shared this with me. I kept the conversation very much on this subject and by the time the meal had finished and we were onto our coffees I decided now was the time to dive in. 'Bella, I'm a medium and I've got a message for you from your mum, darling.' I won't tell you what the message was because I believe that should be private.

'Oh I so needed to hear that; I've been waiting a long time to hear that!' she exclaimed. She was so grateful and elated and went on to tell my why the message was so important to her. Spirit were so wonderful with the evidence they gave her that night along with the message and Bella was over the moon, which made me very happy and obviously the message meant a lot to Bella, but I couldn't help but wonder why the rush to get this message across. It didn't seem so urgent that I needed to work that hard to make sure she got it. But I had done what spirit had wanted me to and that was what was important. So I went home feeling very pleased I was able to do it. Ours is not to reason why.

I did run into Bella a couple of times after that night but beyond saying hello and how are you I thought no more about it. Until that is, a few months later when I heard that Bella had just been diagnosed with dementia, and sadly it was progressing fast which meant she was forgetting people, who they are, and perhaps even that comfort her mother gave her that night would be forgotten. I was so sad to hear this news. Bella wasn't an old lady by any means and to be struck down with this illness was awful. I couldn't shake the message she had received and what would it mean to her now. And then I realised it wasn't the comfort she would get from it now, although she may remember it from time to time, no it was about the comfort it gave her before her memory would be taken from her. Now I know why her mum was so insistent that I gave her that message.

Sadly, it wasn't too long before Bella started to show strong signs of dementia. I'm so glad she was able to have that reunion with her mum and the comfort her mum could give her before her illness took hold. I don't think I'll ever doubt spirit again. They knew why it was important she got that message that night. They knew it was only a matter of time before it wouldn't mean anything to her. Since then I have had many experiences like this one, but on the whole spirit and I have developed an understanding of when I'm working and when I'm not. But they also know if I need to I'll happily clock on again.

Thankfully now I'm able to find some normality in life that I was looking for, well, most of the time, but there are times when I still struggle to balance my working life and my private life but this time it's not because of anything that spirit's doing, no it's because of me. You see I love working with spirit, so when I'm invited to do a mediumship demonstration, give a talk or hold a circle etc., I'm always so happy to say yes, fill my diary up. It's no wonder I get so tired, and then I'm no use to man nor spirit when I'm like that.

I made a statement earlier about 'normality', but you know when I look back on my life I always felt as though normality had completely passed my family by, and I found myself questioning what 'normality' is? What is it I was looking for that would make my life normal? Was my childhood normal? It certainly became that way for me, but not a normal I liked. And I know sexual abuse isn't normal but the feelings of hurt, betrayal, guilt and the lack of trust that it left behind became my normal. The losses I suffered in my early life were mainly people who would be there for a short time and then would walk out; was that normal? When someone passes we can understand that, but when those you care for are there one minute and gone the next without saying goodbye because they chose to move on is something completely different. And I certainly don't class the crap that surrounded my sister's death as normal, and neither was being disowned by my stepfather because of the lies that were told to him before he died. No, normal was definitely not meant to be part of my life, and yes I often asked what I had done to deserve all this.

Don't worry, I'm not feeling sorry for myself, although I didn't realise it until I started to develop as a medium, but before I got here I had agreed to go through every situation I have ever experienced in this lifetime. Yep, I know that sounds crazy but I had agreed to all of this before I ever came back onto this earth. I believe... no, I know through my experiences that we have all lived before so we all have a history of past lives and I'm back here in this lifetime experiencing all these situations because there's some sort of karma to be balanced out. And no, karma isn't about punishment for actions in previous lives contrary to many peoples' opinions. To think of it as a way of punishment is a way of getting our own back by sending out negative vibes to those that have hurt us or made us angry. It's about balancing out and allowing past wrongs to be put right in order to allow evolution to take place within the universe. I believe when we've behaved in such a way that our actions have harmed another, we leave a negative imprint in this world that has a negative effect and prevents evolution to flow correctly.

Yes, my friends, I'm talking about reincarnation, and through my experiences of past life regression I have come to understand so much about why things happen the way they have in this lifetime. If you haven't looked into past life regression I would recommend that you do. Have a little read up on it, you'll be surprised how a lot of what you read makes sense, and it's a great opportunity to learn so much more about who you are and why you react to some situations the way you do without any logical reason. It's a real eye opener.

Talking of eye openers and reactions, my life's experiences have taught me that it's not always life's ups and downs that creates the chaos in our lives. Let's face it, if there's one thing we can guarantee in life, it's that at times something will always come along and throw a spanner in the works of life, and when this happens we can get so defensive and blame life or others when in fact it's actually our reaction that causes the problems and all too often we become a victim of our own thoughts and actions. Don't get me wrong, there are times in life when we are victims of the hurtful behaviours of others and sometimes the hurt others cause can be so hard to get over, and at times their actions can create life changes for us, but does that mean we have to forever be their victims and can't move forward? Does that mean we have to build a wall around us that no-one can break down? Does that mean we have to forever feel the pain and heartache they've caused? You bet your bottom dollar it doesn't! And yet so often that happens. Well, certainly that was what happened to me. I was one of life's victims. I did hold onto all the pain and heartache, I did build a brick wall around me, and all because what happened to me wasn't fair, and it bloody hurt. But all the time I stayed with that thought process I would never be able to make a proper life for myself. All the time I asked, 'Why me?' I was reliving the pain of every bad experience and I was keeping all my bad experiences alive and my perpetrators were still winning.

Of course the 'why me?' attitude got bigger with every experience that I classed as negative, which only ended up taking me in a downward spiral, and everything seemed to be a mountain instead of a molehill and before long every drama turned into a crisis. I tell you I really did wear the T-shirt with the words: 'I'm a victim, take the Mick' written on it, until in the end I got to the point that I had had enough of all the struggles my past was creating in my present. It was time for changes to take place. I know, I know, easier said than done, I hear you say, and you're right, but with the right help and support we can work through anything. I know I really struggled to think that I needed therapy and I would find every reason in the book not to go through all that, but in the end I knew it was the only way forward for me. I knew deep down that this was the only way I was going to be able to let go of all the crap that I had stored up within me for years and leave it all behind me. I can tell you there were times when I came out of a session feeling like I had been run over by a bus, and there were other times I would almost skip along a road as I soaked in that wonderful feeling of relief that I got as I started to let go of all the crap. Yes, on the whole it was all going great, but sometimes it felt like I had to do the impossible in order to let the scars of the past heal.

'And what about forgiveness?' my therapist asked once again

'What about it? Why should I forgive them? What have they ever done to deserve it?' Blah, blah, blah. I used to get so angry that my therapist would suggest I should forgive. How dare she? Why should I let them off the hook? were the thoughts that used to run through my head with such a bitter tone. I wouldn't even contemplate forgiveness, I wanted justice, I wanted those who had hurt me to suffer as much as I did. I went around in a loop over this for years feeling like I was justified not to forgive and of course I was right, but I started to wonder who was the one that was really suffering in the long run. Not them, they've just got on with life, whereas I am still in the same place. I started to realise that I will always end up taking one step forward and five steps back unless I wise up to the liberation of forgiveness, but to do this was going to be my toughest and biggest test yet. Did I feel strong enough to forgive? At that point I didn't know, but I needed to think about it. I can remember the first time I truly contemplated this question without anger, tears or bitterness. It was the end of the day and I felt exhausted and drained, as I had had a counselling session that day and all that we had discussed kept bouncing back in my head. I was really proud of how far I had come, and I was enjoying the new lease of life it was giving me, but I also knew that I kept being yanked back to those painful feelings every now and then, until the penny dropped! Because I wasn't prepared to forgive I wasn't able to be completely free from my past. I was the one that was bringing my past into my present and my future, and that's how it was gonna stay unless I changed.

Trust me, although I knew the next steps I had to take, it really went against the grain to forgive and it felt like those who hurt me were getting away with it. Not justice in my eyes. But I decided to give this forgiveness thing a bit of a chance. After all nothing ventured nothing gained!

The first place to start was with my thought process. I really struggled with this, after all the years I had spent keeping myself safe by holding onto it all, and now I was telling myself to let it all go and move on. At first constantly saying, 'I forgive those who have caused me any hurt, wish them well and move forward,' felt so alien and so false that I never thought it would change the way I felt, but you know what, after a while I noticed that I was starting to feel different about them and the feelings I had held onto for so long had started to subside, just a little but it felt so good and I started to realise just how alive my past still was in my present life. Now that's frightening to think how much control these people still had over my life. Never again was I going to allow that to happen, and once I made that decision and with my new streak of determination I finally took back the control that I had handed over to them years before, and it was surprising just how insignificant the perpetrators became. I realised they just weren't worth wasting my energy on. They couldn't hurt me anymore.

Oh, what a feeling of freedom! For the first time in my life I was really, truly free of the crap that other people had created in my life. Now I can really move forward and leave them way behind me.

Always remember my friends, forgiveness is the key to moving forward and getting your life back.

Chapter 14

WHAT DOESN'T BREAK YOU ONLY MAKES YOU STRONGER

How true that is! I bet you've all been in situations where you're at the end of your tether and think you'll never get through it. And yet we're all still here to tell the tale. Yes, my friends, we're all stronger than we give ourselves credit for. We never see that we deal with situations the best way we can, and most of the time we're dealing with them under stressful circumstances. All too often we believe we're not coping or we're too weak, and in the thick of all the challenges that life can sometimes throw at us it's very hard to see that the struggle we're facing at that time is making us a stronger person. I know for me it was nigh on impossible to believe that at times, and if someone had said to me 'Don't worry this experience will only make you stronger,' I think I would have bitten their head off big time! I wouldn't have been able to see at that time why there would be a need for me to be 'made stronger'. I wouldn't have been able to see what purpose experiencing this pain and heartache would bring, and to be honest, I wouldn't have given a hoot. I just wanted it all to go away. I wanted my Dad back.

Life is full of experiences and we're never going to avoid the hard painful ones, no matter how hard we try, and we have to try and learn from them otherwise it's all been a pointless exercise, and I can guarantee we will endure the same kind of experiences again and again. Have you ever noticed how some people experience the same kind of challenges in their life frequently? That's because they haven't learnt from it, which means they will continue to attract the same kind of bad situations or relationships, etc. to them.

Yep, we've got to learn from every situation we're faced with or we could end up with a broken spirit.

So when I look back at the experiences in my life, do I think I've learnt? Well putting it bluntly, I bloody well hope so! Would I live it all again? Hmm, that's a difficult one to answer. Even though I know it's made me stronger, to endure all that pain and suffering again would be a hard task, and yet deep down inside of me I know it's only through all that I've endured in my life that I understand more about life now. Yes I know, corny, but true! No longer do I have those moments when I question why I'm on this earth or if I have the right to be here, because that's how I felt for so long. I saw myself as an excuse for a human being. As I look back I remember those days as being so dark, so emotionally frightening, and now so very, very distant, thank goodness. Now I wake up every morning counting my blessings for all that I have in my life and for all that I have survived, and I like to think that I have learnt how to live a better life.

When my sister passed I always said her legacy to me was the gift of life. She made me realise nothing in this life is worth destroying ourselves over; that wasn't why we were put on this earth. My sister was a great teacher when she was alive ,which I carry in my heart, and she's taught me as much through her passing. She helped me to let go and learn how to be free. She taught me if I could survive her passing I could survive anything, and I truly believe that she guided me along the path I needed to take for my next stages in life. When my mother passed, the loss and grief had a natural flow because there were no bad circumstances, no dramas, just her passing into the next transition, and it taught me that death is the most natural part of life, and it's the one thing in life that's guaranteed and should not to be feared. But just because it was a natural passing doesn't mean to say that I miss her any the less than I do my sister. I miss her every day, but I could accept easier that it was her time. But with Dad's passing, it was very different. Our relationship had been damaged with no opportunity to make the peace between us. I was deeply worried that he passed over thinking I didn't love him, that I didn't care for him, which couldn't be further from the truth. He died confused, angry and bitter, and that broke my heart. And because of my sadness and grief I had forgotten all the messages that I had given from spirit to their loved ones reassuring them that all they suffered before they passed over has now gone and they are at peace. It's funny really, although we weren't blood relatives, we were very alike. Both stubborn, both proud and both hot headed. Sometimes I regret letting these traits in me get in the way of our relationship, but I don't believe he would have wanted our relationship to be any other way. He had a sparring partner and he loved that!

My own pain of what had happened in his last few months had clouded all of that, but thankfully spirit, my guides, my family and friends in spirit were there to gently remind me and support me through the hard times. Even Dad has come through on many occasions and the peace has been made between us. Deep down I would love to have had that peace that Dad and I feel now to have happened before he passed, but as we can't change the way things happen in our life, this is good enough, and to be fair to Dad, a man that didn't believe 'in this kind of stuff' until the end of his life. His messages have been so comforting to know that he's made the effort to come through and make sure I knew that he now understands what really happened, which only goes to show there are some things in this life that can't be broken and bonds are one of them. Dad and I may have been at odds before he passed but the love we had for each other was stronger than we even realised, we just had to go beyond what's important in this material world and cherish what's important in our spiritual world, and that my friends is love. It hasn't always felt like I have been on the right path in life and that's been pretty scary, but I understand now that the right path isn't always the easiest, but if we trust in spirit, our guides and teachers, they will make sure there isn't a hurdle we can't jump over.

It's funny how life turns out for us. I never had a plan set out to be a medium. I never planned on standing in front of people, connecting with their loved ones in spirit and delivering messages to them, and never in a million years thought I would be investigating spooky castles, houses, pubs etc., but here I am doing all of this and loving every minute of it. Thankfully spirit had plans for me and they made sure somehow in some way I was in the right place at the right time to guide me to where I am now. Thank you spirit for never giving up on me and for being so patient with me. You got me there in the end!

So where to next? God only knows – literally! But I do know this, wherever it is, whatever it involves, and whatever I face, it won't break me! I'm a survivor, as I know all of you are too. Just take a look back at all that you've been up against and all the obstacles you've overcome in your past. Now tell me you're not a survivor! Yes, there will always be times when our dreams, goals and hopes will be dashed, that's part of life, but giving in isn't an option for us survivors. My life has changed in so many ways over the last decade, and as you now know, some of these changes have been very, very challenging and I spent a lot of time fighting them, but for all that, some of the changes that came from my experiences have had some very positive outcomes, even if I didn't plan them.

I really hope by me sharing my experiences it has helped to reach any part of you that has felt like giving up. Always remember my friends, you're being supported and you're going to get through any challenge you face because you're never alone.

And for any budding mediums out there, don't question your abilities, don't do yourself down, just get out there and find a place that's right for you to develop those hidden abilities and go for it!

* * * *